Anti-Money Laundering

Anti-Money Laundering

A practical guide to reducing organizational risk

Rose Chapman

KoganPage

First published in Great Britain and the United States in 2018 by Kogan Page Limited

2nd Floor, 45 Gee Street
London EC1V 3RS
United Kingdom

c/o Martin P Hill Consulting
122 W 27th St, 10th Floor
New York NY 10001
USA

4737/23 Ansari Road
Daryaganj
New Delhi 110002
India

www.koganpage.com

ISBN 978 0 7494 8189 6
E-ISBN 978 0 7494 8190 2

British Library Cataloguing-in-Publication Data

A CIP record for this book is available from the British Library.

Library of Congress Cataloging-in-Publication Data

CIP data is available.

Library of Congress Control Number: 2018013613

Typeset by Integra Software Services, Pondicherry
Print production managed by Jellyfish
Printed and bound by CPI Group (UK) Ltd, Croydon, CR0 4YY

Dedicated to the memory of Andy Bomphrey

CONTENTS

ABOUT THE AUTHOR

Rose Chapman is the Global Head of Compliance and Ethics (C&E) at Travelport Inc. An Anti-Money Laundering and Compliance professional with around 20 years' experience in financial services and international corporate environments, she held the role of Financial Services Authority Controlled Functions of Compliance Officer (CF10) and Money Laundering Reporting Officer (CF11) for a number of years before achieving a Masters of Law distinction in International Corporate Governance, Financial Regulation and Economic Law at the Institute of Advanced Legal Studies, University of London. Rose then moved on to the world of technology and digital payment solutions. Rose has a penchant for developing anti-money laundering and compliance systems and controls by evolution rather than revolution ahead of the game and to suit the firm. It's a mission.

DISCLAIMER

ACKNOWLEDGEMENTS AND DEDICATION

In writing this book I would like to thank Rachel Cropper-Mawer, Partner at DAC Beachcroft LLP, for her welcome feedback and valuable input, and David Chamberlain for his review of the drafts with the careful eye of an experienced book printing professional. It is always helpful to have a candid review of drafts when writing and I could not have hoped for better allies than Rachel and David.

I would like to dedicate this book to the memory of Andy Bomphrey, who gave me the opportunity to join his Compliance team at Pearl Assurance when I returned to work as his temporary PA over 20 years ago. Andy offered me the opportunity of progression in the firm as a Compliance Adviser and arranged for me to take professional qualifications to underpin my new Compliance role. He moved me into the 'jungle' of Compliance Operations and then Compliance Developments, where I learnt to study legislation and make the best of it for the benefit of the firm years before embarking on my Masters in Law. Without Andy's support, as a mother returning to full-time work after 12 years of childcare, I could easily have missed out on career opportunities. It is highly likely that without it I would never have become a Money Laundering Reporting Officer and Compliance Officer holding Controlled Functions 10 and 11 in the UK, or moved on to become responsible globally for Compliance and Ethics in an organization operating in well over a hundred countries in the world.

Thank you, Andy.

LIST OF ABBREVIATIONS

1MLD	First European Union Anti-Money Laundering Directive
2MLD	Second European Union Anti-Money Laundering Directive
3MLD	Third European Union Anti-Money Laundering Directive
4MLD	Fourth European Union Anti-Money Laundering Directive
5MLD	Fifth European Union Anti-Money Laundering Directive
9/11	Attack on the World Trade Center, 11 September 2001
ABC	Anti Bribery and Corruption
AML	Anti-Money Laundering
BCCI	Bank of Credit and Commerce International
BoE	Bank of England
CBRC	China Banking Regulatory Commission
CDD	Client Due Diligence
CEO	Chief Executive Officer
CF	Controlled Function
CFA	UK Criminal Finances Act 2017
CRA	Customer Risk Assessment
CTF	Counter-Terrorist Financing
CV	Curriculum Vitae
DIFC	Dubai International Financial Centre
DNFBP	Designated Non-Financial Businesses and Professions
DoJ	US Department of Justice
EDD	Enhanced Due Diligence
Egmont Group	The Egmont Group of Financial Intelligence Units
ESA	European Supervisory Authority

EU	European Union
FATF	Financial Action Task Force
FCA	Financial Conduct Authority
FCPA	Foreign Corrupt Practices Act 1977
FIU	Financial Intelligence Unit
FSA	Financial Services Authority
FSMA	Financial Services and Markets Act 2000
FSTB	Financial Services and Treasury Bureau
GDPR	General Data Privacy Regulation
GPML	Global Programme Against Money Laundering
HMRC	Her Majesty's Revenue and Customs
HR	Human Resources
HSBC	Hong Kong and Shanghai Banking Corporation/HSBC Private Bank
IMF	International Monetary Fund
IPO	Initial Public Offering
ISO	Independent Sales Organization
IT	Information Technology
KYC	Know Your Customer
Lancore	Lancore Services Ltd
M&A	Merger and Acquisition
MEA	Mallards Estate Agency
MENA	Middle East and North Africa
MLRO	Money Laundering Reporting Officer
MNE	Multinational Enterprise
NGO	Non-governmental Organization
OCC	Office of the Comptroller of the Currency
OECD	Organization for Economic Co-operation and Development
OFAC	Office of Foreign Asset Control
PA	Personal Assistant
PEP	Politically Exposed Person
POCA	Proceeds of Crime Act 2002
R16	Recommendation 16 of the Financial Action Task Force

RO	Responsible Officer
SAR	Suspicious Activity Report
SBUK	Sonali Bank UK
SDD	Simplified Due Diligence
SEC	United States Securities and Exchange Commission
SOCA	Serious Organized Crime Agency
SOX	Sarbanes-Oxley Act 2002
SR	Special Recommendation of the Financial Action Task Force
TCSPs	Trust and Company Service Providers
Telia	Telia Company AB
TI	Transparency International
UBO	Ultimate Beneficial Owner
UK	United Kingdom
UN	United Nations
UNODC	United Nations Office on Drugs and Crime
USA	United States of America
Yonge	Yonge Enterprise (Group) Co Ltd

A NOTE BEFORE YOU BEGIN

In different jurisdictions there are various terms used for the person who is responsible for anti-money laundering (AML) in an organization. In the UK it is the Money Laundering Reporting Officer, or the Nominated Officer. Other terms include the Responsible Officer, and all of these terms are used in this book to denote the person responsible for AML.

Introduction

Money laundering is a growth industry that has taken on a new life online in recent years, proliferating fraud via the internet and resulting in more industries and professional services being subject to anti-money laundering (AML) regulation. There is opportunity and the need for organizations to engage more skilful and knowledgeable people to attend to money laundering prevention, which spans across new industries and anywhere on earth where the intention is for organizations to engage in international trade.

This book is a practical guide to reducing the risk of an organization being used as a vehicle by criminals laundering the proceeds of crime. Its intention is to arm you with the informational tools you need to establish, improve or enhance the AML controls in your organization, whether its reach is local or international.

The book is written for emerging AML professionals at all levels of an organization, whether they are there because of selected career development, or by being unintentionally caught in the path of regulatory scope-creep, which increasingly pulls resource into the international battle against money laundering. It is also written for those established AML professionals in the regulated sphere seeking to develop a holistic view of the steps their organization may need to take to better establish AML controls. The book provides a broadened view outside of the role of many AML professionals who may need to extend their knowledge of implementing an AML control environment in readiness for a promotion or a larger remit in their current role.

What is money laundering?

Money laundering is activity that takes place following a criminal act of, say, drug trafficking, corruption, theft, fraud, tax evasion or bribery to make illegal monetary gains look like franked, or clean money, which the criminal can then use safely and without detection. So, essentially, money laundering is not the initial crime itself. A crime of theft, fraud or drug smuggling is perpetrated, which is the predicate crime, and criminals working through the process of disguising the money into seemingly legitimate funds is the money laundering. Doing this well is such a focus for the money launderer that complex arrangements may be devised, and more than five steps between carrying out the predicate crime and benefiting from its proceeds would not be unusual. Having said that, money laundering does not have to be complex at all. It can be as simple as a thief spending the money stolen from a wallet on goods on the high street, using a stolen item for his or her own benefit, or carrying out work for cash and spending it without paying taxes. As soon as benefits are drawn from the proceeds of crime there is money laundering.

Money laundering activity is traditionally explained in the three separate activities of placement, layering and integration, and otherwise legitimate organizations are vulnerable to being used by criminals to launder money at each stage. *Placement* is the first step, where the proceeds of crime are introduced to the laundering process. They may be placed in a bank account or other financial instrument, from where they can be forwarded to others. *Layering* comes next in the traditional explanation, where funds are moved around financial services vehicles, such as from a fully paid insurance product that is cancelled quickly and then transferred straight into an investment product from the legitimate insurance source. The aim is for the bank or investment house to link the name of the insurer with a legitimate source of funds and by doing this the money launderer puts distance between the criminal act and the funds gained from it. Lastly comes the *integration process*. Now money launderers have distanced the funds from criminality, they can withdraw it as seemingly legitimate funds and more safely purchase retail goods or engage in activities of their choice and benefit from their criminal activity.

This definition, although helpful, does not cover the many faces of money laundering, and other instances include:

- Facilitation of tax evasion.
- Giving cash payments for high-value goods.
- Hiding beneficial ownership of funds in shell companies.

- Structuring, or 'smurfing' large amounts of cash into smaller deposits and then withdrawing them as legitimate funds.
- Mixing legally obtained funds with criminal money in cash-based businesses, such as florist shops, restaurants or launderettes.
- Casino and gambling laundering, where criminals place cash bets and claim the winnings as clean funds from the betting organization into their bank account.

Always remember: there is no need to have money for there to be money laundering. Any benefit derived from crime counts. For example:

> Ron, the owner of a heavy goods vehicle, is driving along a country road one evening when he sees that a crop of baled hay has been left in a field. It has been a spring of little rain and the hay price is high. After darkness falls Ron takes helpers and fills his vehicle with bales of hay that he drives the next day to a rural area where there is a stable of racehorses. The stable manager welcomes Ron and pays the agreed price for the hay he has ordered, which he offsets from the cost of keeping a horse on behalf of Ron's racing syndicate. He does not question the origin of his hay delivery.
>
> Deepak works in a factory as a quality control operative for a training shoe manufacturer. He has the authority to deem the shoes unfit for sale should they have flaws. Deepak is a drug addict and income from his day job is not sufficient to supply drugs to satisfy his habit, so he has come to a convenient arrangement with the drugs dealer, who will exchange the drugs Deepak consumes per week for five pairs of designer training shoes. This results in Deepak being a thief, and the drugs dealer a criminal on two counts: supplying drugs, and laundering the proceeds of crime.

Money laundering in cyberspace

There is certainly a significant amount of online fraud, including ransomware attacks and money laundering. Ransomware attacks, where cybercriminals take over computers of whole organizations, are on such a scale that they receive high profile publicity. However, frauds where individuals are targeted, for example via their e-mail account and then led to divulge their bank account details or passwords are also prevalent. They get plenty of publicity and regulatory regimes are expanding all the time to include online activity. In the UK for example, Her Majesty's Revenue & Customs (HMRC) expanded its list of types of business that should register under money laundering regulations. From 26 June 2017 the seven types include three types of online business: money service businesses, bill payment service providers, and telecommunication, digital and IT payment service providers.

So long as our organizations are not the target, clarification via regulatory updates and current cases are good news for AML professionals as we develop our control environment, as there is plenty of information out there to help us! This book explores emerging AML online risks as well as those in the physical world in establishing controls to help reduce both online and physical money laundering risks in our organizations.

Where in the world are AML controls implemented?

Wherever your organization is in the world today, to operate effectively in the international market AML controls are increasingly a must have for doing business. Countries that were staunchly nationalistic and resistant to the implementation of AML controls are increasingly moving towards them now, although the challenge from adherents to local cultural norms can be fierce and sustained. In this book we will consider a selection of these norms, some giving protection for the powerful, some hiding beneficial ownership and others where speeding the course of government control arrangements by way of facilitation payments is common. There are governments that have moved from zero to hero on the implementation of AML and anti-bribery legislation, and the effects of such precipitous change to satisfy AML requirements are explored too. Fortunately, there are excellent opportunities to network internationally in AML, for governments, mostly via their Financial Intelligence Units (FIUs) and the international best practice bodies such as the Wolfsberg Group of banks.

For you as an AML professional, there are organizations that make it their business to disseminate AML knowledge and create interest groups of students and alumni such as the International Compliance Association. High profile cases where bribery and money laundering are widely discussed, new and proposed legislation and organizations such as Transparency International and the Financial Action Task Force (FATF) provide good sources of information. These international views compared to your local legislation will show you what needs to be done to reduce the AML risk in your organization and keep ahead of the curve. You just need to know where to look to find it all, which this book will help you to do.

So, AML controls are defined in local legislation?

Yes they are, but, and this is a golden 'but' for all AML professionals, the core principles and requirements are all internationally defined. They come from one source, which is a huge advantage for you should you wish to work internationally. As we will see, the fight against money laundering is a long and expanding battle over decades, strategically developing with the emergence of new threats, but whether you are in Melbourne or London, Singapore or Washington, the fundamental AML requirements are the same, defined in international best practice.

What is the source of the core AML principles?

The source of AML best practice and requirements is the 40 Recommendations introduced by the FATF, formed by members of the Organization for Economic Co-operation and Development (OECD) in 1989. These recommendations, first introduced in 1990, have been updated over time, and increasingly they are being enacted into local legislation and regulation. They provide a working template for the AML professional to apply locally, and as legislation the world over aims to provide local controls to adhere to those 40 Recommendations, this book is equally relevant to implementing local controls as it is to operating in the international sphere. It gives insight into elements that can be taken to establish appropriate controls to manage the money laundering risks of your organization, and provides guidance to help you spot vulnerabilities and prevent your organization being used as a vehicle to launder the proceeds of crime.

As always, implemented laws differ amongst jurisdictions, but the globally applicable AML control structure that this book describes, which can be adopted and adapted to local needs by breaking it down into its component parts, includes:

1. Governance and control environment.
2. Employee hiring, training and management.
3. Business, product, geography and client demographic risk assessment.
4. Client due diligence.
5. Ongoing monitoring and transaction screening of client activity.
6. Data management and flows of information.
7. Guidance and support to the business.
8. Internal and external investigations.
9. Holistic monitoring and improvement of the system, using the AML strategy wheel.

AML controls are just for financial services companies, aren't they?

Controls on the movement of money started in the financial services sector to stop the funds derived from drug trafficking crossing borders, but the money itself is laundered in the business and personal lives of criminals, and in this way the proceeds of crime may pervade the otherwise legal income or activity of an organization. For example, the proceeds of crime may pervade real estate, company services, accountancy and legal advice – those activities to where anti-money laundering controls have spread. Organizations may also, knowingly or unknowingly, give criminals access to their services in cash-rich businesses such as restaurants or launderettes, or by sharing payment services merchant access to the financial system, giving rise to the risk of being an accessory to a crime. Artworks, diamonds and historical artefacts of high worth can all be the 'currency' of the money launderer rather than money itself.

The introduction of new legislation, including the European Union's Fourth Money Laundering Directive (4MLD), spreads the reach of financial services regulation ever wider and encourages if not mandates the adoption of a risk-based approach for AML activities in the financial and professional services industries. 4MLD very much widens the focus of money laundering control beyond the financial services sector, and in its 'Action plan for anti-money laundering and counter-terrorist finance' published in April 2016, the British Government acknowledges that money laundering and terrorist financing undermine the integrity of financial institutions and markets, enable criminals to hide, store and benefit from the proceeds of their crime, and enable terrorist groups to function, recruit and commit terrorist acts. We believe that in the same way that newly obliged organizations can learn from those with established AML controls, each country can benefit from the improvements in legislation taking place in others. Observation of the progress of other jurisdictions saves time and local development costs in coming to an appropriate starting point from which local regulations can be implemented. This book sets out the controls that organizations, established or newly obliged, have to put in place to satisfy the 40 Recommendations of FATF to prevent them being used for money laundering. These include:

- Assessment of the risk of your organization being used as a vehicle for money laundering by criminals.
- Carrying out checks to determine the identity of your customers where they are natural persons.
- Checking the identity of the ultimate, or beneficial, owner of corporates and partnerships with which you are doing business.
- Having management control systems in place in your organization.
- Training your employees so that they are aware of AML regulations.
- Monitoring customer activity in the use of the services of your organization.

- Keeping adequate records of all required activities, including customer identity, beneficial ownership, financial transactions and governance controls such as policies, procedures and processes.
- Reporting suspicious activity to your local country FIU.

If you are working in a newly obliged organization, you may be looking for, or looking to become, an AML 'gatekeeper' and you will need to have in place appropriate controls from the selection above. The list of obliged organizations currently includes:

- auditors, external accountants and tax advisers;
- credit institutions;
- estate agents and letting agents;
- financial institutions;
- notaries and other legal professionals;
- providers of gambling services;
- traders in goods making or receiving payments above €10,000;
- trusts and company service providers.

This list is expanding as money launderers find it more difficult to launder their criminal funds using financial services vehicles, and will continue to strategically move into new industries and oblige new gatekeepers to take action as FIUs find criminal funds being laundered in new ways.

What risks remain if an organization does not adopt AML controls?

The risk to an organization of being party to money laundering is in the knowledge or suspicion that goods or money have been derived from criminal activity, and are the proceeds of crime. Organizations can be set up specifically to assist in money laundering activities, or be infiltrated by criminals who use its systems to launder the proceeds of crime. In *The Puppet Masters*, the World Bank reviewed around 150 cases and found that they shared a number of common characteristics. In the vast majority of them:

- a corporate vehicle was misused to hide the money trail;
- the corporate vehicle in question was a company or corporation;
- the proceeds and instruments of corruption consisted of funds in a bank account; and
- in cases where the ownership information was available, the corporate vehicle in question was established or managed by a professional intermediary. (van der Does de Willebois *et al,* 2011)

The corporate vehicles created or misused to conceal the proceeds of 'grand corruption', ie corruption on an enormous scale, runs to an estimated US$40 billion per annum. Providers of legal, financial and administrative (management) services, including banks, financial institutions, lawyers, accountants, and other professionals that are known as trust and company service providers (TCSPs), are shown to facilitate money laundering schemes. All of this is happening within regulated organizations. Perhaps trusted employees are using yours to launder the proceeds of crime right now! Anyone who knows or suspects that this is the case and deals with those goods or money, is carrying out money laundering activity. No knowledge of the crime or the criminals is necessary to be guilty of money laundering, and whether or not an organization is in the ever-widening regulated sector, awareness of what money laundering looks like and putting in place steps to prevent it is key to reducing operational risk.

There are now many examples of companies, such as the Rolls Royce case of 2017, which clearly show the financial and reputational risks that an organization takes when it leaves itself open to laundering the proceeds of crime. The eye-watering fines imposed in the United States and the United Kingdom are a clear indication that even where regulators historically have not imposed significant sanctions, increasingly they will not stop at minor penalties for which companies can easily provision. They are change-makers. After several previous regulatory interventions and the 2012 case that revealed, literally, the movement of vans full of bank notes over the border from Mexico to the United States, the Hong Kong and Shanghai Banking Corporation (HSBC) became subject to ongoing intrusive regulatory scrutiny that continues years later. The risks of failing to be aware of and control money laundering risk affect smaller organizations also, and where financial penalties are applied they may have a greater impact to their ongoing operations.

How might I benefit by reading more?

AML compliance is a growth profession, with opportunities to develop a career path of real benefit to legitimate business activity. This book highlights the essential elements of how that might be achieved by exploring the experience of financial and professional services organizations. It offers a governance structure to benefit compliance adherence in an organization and so reduce its operational risk well beyond money laundering, providing a template for establishing robust internal controls. If you find yourself at the forefront of cultural change in your organization or region that is taking place today, you will gain insight into strategies to overcome the sometimes immense challenges AML professionals face in establishing appropriate de-risking AML controls. You will benefit by identifying the organizational procedures necessary at the point of interaction with third parties to establish client relationships and provide services, the monitoring of activity in those relationships, the training and awareness required by relevant employees to identify money laundering activity, and gain insight into liaison with governmental authorities in reporting and assisting in investigations. Case studies are drawn from a range of countries, and those that this book explores draw out the steps organizations can take in illustrations of success and failure, to help you de-risk your organization from a money laundering perspective and strengthen the compliance culture.

References

Directive (EU) 2015/849 of The European Parliament and of The Council of 20 May 2015 on the prevention of the use of the financial system for the purposes of money laundering or terrorist financing, amending Regulation (EU) No 648/2012 of the European Parliament and of the Council, and repealing Directive 2005/60/EC of the European Parliament and of the Council and Commission Directive 2006/70/EC (Fourth Money Laundering Directive)

Serious Fraud Office v Rolls Royce PLC and Rolls Royce Energy Systems Inc (2017) U20170036 (QB); see also Williams-Grut, O (2017) *Egregious Criminality Over Decades: Judge's damning verdict on the Rolls-Royce bribery case,* 18/1, available at: http://uk.businessinsider.com/rolls-royce-pays-671-million-to-settle-bribery-and-corruption-probes-2017-1?r=US&IR=T (last accessed 23 January 2018)

van der Does de Willebois, E, Halter, E M, Harrison, R A, Park, Ji Won, Sharman, J C (2011) *The Puppet Masters. How the corrupt use legal structures to hide stolen assets and what to do about it. Stolen asset recovery initiative*, The World Bank, available at: https://star.worldbank.org/star/sites/star/files/puppetmastersv1.pdf (last accessed 23 January 2018)

Reaction 01

The rise of anti-money laundering and counter-terrorist financing activity

Although financial crime and the laundering of its proceeds go back through history, the requirement to establish controls to prevent criminals laundering money is relatively recent. This chapter will set the scene of anti-money laundering (AML) regulatory development and introduce the players whose collaboration across the divides of national boundaries has been effective in producing a global AML strategy. It is this that assists AML professionals to transport their skills, giving opportunities to build an international career as more countries seek to implement or improve their AML regulatory controls. There is a wealth of information available online, and some of the most notable websites are shown at the end of this chapter, which will cover:

- Defining money laundering.
- The reactive nature of regulatory development.
- Source of anti-money laundering and counter-terrorist financing controls: the Financial Action Task Force.
- The players involved in developing AML and CTF controls.
- Keeping up to date: notable website addresses.

Defining money laundering

Money laundering is the movement or use of the benefits of criminal activity. It includes disguising the source of currency, goods or property derived from the crime so that the criminals can benefit securely from it. The avoidance of leaving a trail back to the crime provides the activity of money laundering, as does benefiting from the crime by utilizing its proceeds directly.

Money laundering is broadly not the initial, 'predicate' crime. A crime of, say, fraud, theft, drug dealing, is committed, and the very next thing the criminal does with the money or goods gained through that crime is money laundering in whatever form that takes. Not all crimes generate funds in cash that need to be placed into the financial system; for an example of this see Case Study 1.1.

CASE STUDY 1.1: Money laundering without any money

An investigation at a major US airport revealed that rather than handing in items left behind by travellers, aeroplane maintenance workers were stealing them in a widespread theft ring involving numerous employees and supervisors who were targeting such items. These items could be money, children's toys, or expensive tablets including iPads, Kindles and other electronic devices. Although some of these items were found for sale in local pawn shops, they were also being stolen for the thieves' own use. Police told CNN that the cleaners and maintenance workers were stealing the items as they could not afford to buy them for themselves. Some iPhones and iPads were tracked to the homes of employees using Apple's Find My iPhone option. One of the thieves told police that she took the items because it was easy and no one was watching, offering her a virtual invitation to steal. (CNN, 2016)

Questions

1. Is appropriate management control and oversight given to employees of your organization to minimize the opportunity of theft?
2. Does that control extend to those who are the least well paid?
3. What is the balance of trust v control that is applied to employees and contractors with access to your organization?

In Case Study 1.1, economic factors combined with opportunity led employees to steal expensive items from airline passengers. This crime predicates the money laundering process. As soon as the thief starts using the proceeds of the crime, such as an iPad for his or her own use, that person is money laundering even though no money is involved.

The 'three-stage money laundering process' provides a useful and clear explanation of how money that is recognizable as the proceeds of crime can be cleaned through the financial system until it appears to be legitimate. The three-step process of placement, layering and integration works like this:

1. *Placement:* placing criminal or dirty money into an account or financial vehicle.
2. *Layering:* moving the money across financial vehicles multiple times.
3. *Integration:* spending the money now cleaned by placement and layering in the public domain, perhaps on a luxury house or classic car.

From this familiar three-step process, one can be led to believe that only financial institutions are at risk from being used for money laundering purposes by criminals. This is not always the case: although the financial sector is very attractive to criminals for laundering money, and placement, layering and integration are very useful in explaining money laundering, it is more and more difficult for criminals to launder money this way due to AML regulation. AML regulation began in the financial services industry, but its reach continues to broaden out, drawing more organizations into the regulated sector as criminals seek to find new ways to launder the proceeds of their crimes. Obliged entities can now be found in real estate, gambling and high-value goods. Whether part of the expanded regulated sector or not, many organizations can learn from the principles used in AML regulation to inform risk assessments of their own activities, thereby reducing risk and improving corporate governance.

AML controls help to establish where money coming into your business originates. In terrorist financing, the investigator is looking at where the money is going. Is it going to fund terrorist acts via a charity, for instance? Differentiating factors between money launderers and terrorist financing also includes the criminals' motivation. Money launderers are identified as greedy people who want to make money and are happy to use financial and other organizations to do so. These organizations also make money through providing their services, and sometimes incentivize sales people to bring in new business while operating weak client due diligence (CDD) controls, such as in the case of Coutts Bank in the United Kingdom in Case Study 1.2. (For more on CDD, see Chapter 4.)

CASE STUDY 1.2: Weak CDD benefiting a regulated entity

Coutts is a bank catering for the needs of wealthy customers, and is part of the Royal Bank of Scotland group of companies. In March 2012 the UK Financial Services Authority (now the Financial Conduct Authority) imposed a fine of £8.75 million on Coutts because, 'It failed to take reasonable care to establish and maintain effective anti-money laundering (AML) systems and controls in relation to... high-risk customers.' An extract from the Final Notice reads:

> Coutts' failings merit the imposition of a significant financial penalty. The FSA considers the failings to be particularly serious because:
>
> i Coutts is a high profile bank with a leading position in the private banking market and is a gateway to the UK financial system for high net worth international customers. It was particularly important, therefore, that Coutts had robust systems and controls to prevent and detect money laundering;
>
> ii the markets and customers that the Firm was targeting included certain jurisdictions with AML requirements which were not equivalent to those in the UK and which carried an inherently high risk in respect of money laundering;
>
> iii the Firm provided financial services to a large number of high-risk customers, the number of which approximately doubled during the Relevant Period, and it handled considerable sums of money on behalf of those customers;
>
> iv the failings persisted for a period of almost three years;
>
> v the failings were not identified by the Firm. (FCA, 2012)

Doubtless Coutts was also reaping profits in terms of fees for services from these high-risk customers during that time.

Questions

1 Does your organization shy away from collecting information to prove identity when a client has the potential to provide greater profitability?

2 What training is given to sales people about taking on new clients?

3 How are new client relationships monitored in your organization?

4 Do you have a reporting mechanism whereby an employee can raise concerns for higher-risk clients?

In contrast to money launderers, terrorists tend to spend very little money to purchase the implements they use in their attacks. For example, in 2017 Police Constable Keith Palmer was stabbed in a terrorist attack while guarding the entrance to the UK's Houses of Parliament. The terrorist assailant used a single kitchen knife for the attack, purchased from a high street store along with his groceries for the week, and the knife was used to deadly effect. The small amount of spend involved to perpetrate such acts makes it very difficult to detect terrorist activity using AML controls.

The reactive nature of regulatory development

In AML as well as other regulatory formation, development is essentially reactive. When high profile money laundering convictions occur there is likely to be regulatory change with the aim of preventing that scenario happening again. See what happened when US giant Enron was found to be engaged in false accounting, in Case Study 1.3.

CASE STUDY 1.3: Reactive regulatory development

Prior to this scandal, Enron was a global corporation based in the United States with activities in the provision of electricity and gas in the energy market. It also provided financial and risk management services to customers around the world. In November 2001, it emerged that Enron had overstated its earnings by several hundred million dollars. Enron's executives were the architects of false accounting to hide losses and, before the scandal broke, they sold company shares at a value of up to $90.75 per share. The value dropped to just $0.67 by

January 2002, and fraud charges followed. Enron's auditors, Arthur Anderson, were pressured by Enron executives to ignore the accounting issues. Neither company survived. On investigation, the US Securities and Exchange Commission recommended the implementation of new and far-reaching controls. These were brought together in the Sarbanes-Oxley Act 2002 (SOX), which mandates that senior management must certify the accuracy of company financial reporting. The internal controls necessary to do this are far-reaching for US listed companies, and it requires considerable resources to establish and maintain the necessary internal control to meet the requirements (SEC v Kenneth L Lay, Jeffrey K Skilling, Richard A Causey, 2004).

Questions

1 In your jurisdiction, are you aware of organizations that appear to consider themselves unhampered by local laws?

2 How is senior management structured within your organization? Do you think that your executives may be able to push the boundaries of corporate activity beyond regulatory controls?

3 Seek to identify four financial controls in your organization, controls that place a check on the passage of funds internally or externally.

Enron is just one case amongst many that have driven regulatory reform in the area of financial crime. The 2014 Organized Crime and Corruption Reporting Project reported that huge amounts of apparently illicit money has been found to be flowing from Russia into European countries using shell companies, some set up in the UK. This massive amount of money, estimated at around US$20.8 billion, was moved using a complex criminal financial vehicle termed the 'Russian laundromat' (OCCRP, 2017) which involved laundering the money using several well-known banks. This is an example of the sort of finding that leads to regulatory change and the extension of AML requirements to previously unregulated industries.

The reactive nature of AML regulatory development may seem chaotic, but its organizational core is not. Unlike the evolution of regulatory compliance in financial services, which is diverse, having its roots in local countries, the development of AML compliance is a broadly unified story, as described below. Some countries embraced and implemented new legislation and controls early, keen for change, and others have resisted change until it became a prerequisite for full engagement in global finance and other services. The original international bodies that introduced AML regulation still exist, and they are instrumental in guiding the direction of AML regulation today.

Source of AML and CTF controls: The Financial Action Task Force

The increase in AML activity was initiated by members of the Organization for Economic Co-operation and Development (OECD), which wanted to stem the flow of drug money across their borders. Realizing that collective action was more likely to have a greater impact, countries combined their efforts and the core controls on drug trafficking were developed by an organization created by OECD members in 1989: the Financial Action Task Force (FATF).

Although AML legislation is implemented by regulators and organizations the world over with local variation, the core controls have developed along a coordinated and steady international path, with FATF at their centre. FATF members established the first Financial Intelligence Units (FIUs) in each of their countries as local hubs of AML coordination. The role of each FIU is to assess and process suspicious activity reports (SARs) and cooperate with both financial institutions and law enforcement in the jurisdiction, as well as engaging in cross-border liaison with other FIUs to share their expertise and exchange information. As the FIUs began to communicate with each other and share information, trust between them grew and their interaction started to become more useful in terms of content, speed and impact.

These efforts to throw impediments in the path of drug traffickers is the source of AML activity, to prevent them from benefiting from the profits made by ruining the lives of countless people by addiction to the drugs they sell, and these controls have to evolve with the times to retain their relevance. The way that money moves across borders has changed beyond recognition since 1989, when FATF was created. In the days before computers and online banking, money laundering was part of the physical world, like the post before e-mail, and the early FATF members created international standards on combating money laundering that were relevant to the perceived threats of their era. Movement of laundered dollar bills crossing borders (which we will encounter in Case Study 8.2) still happens, but less so with the greater efficiency and speed of electronic transfers.

FATF is the primary source of guidance and the leading AML organization globally, and its entire objective is the development and promotion of national and international strategies to combat money laundering. In a move that spreads the word of money laundering awareness to ever more people and nations, FATF produces typologies, which give examples of money laundering themes and cases. There is a wealth of information on AML development available online; the FATF website address among others is shown at the end of this chapter.

FATF functions include providing recommendations and guidance to countries in the development of their AML regulatory regime, including reform of country-specific legislative provisions. Country compliance assessment also forms part of FATF activity via its mutual evaluation process. It is an essential driver of the AML control environment as country analysis provides a benchmark for compliance amongst competitor economies. Onsite evaluations by representatives nominated by FATF are also carried out, as are the less demanding annual self-assessment exercises.

FATF 40 Recommendations

The original FATF Recommendations were published as 'international standards on combating money laundering and the financing of terrorism and proliferation of weapons of mass destruction' in 1990. They are updated to remain current as advances in communications and banking technology speed the flow of criminal funds transfers across the globe. The international FIU network established by FATF fuelled development of controls, asking: 'What steps can we take together to stop money laundering, in and across the borders of our nations?' This is the simplicity and clarity of AML in terms of guidance across the globe. Wherever the enquirer is based, there is one source to provide the core information needed to guide jurisdictions and inform organizations on how to combat money laundering: FATF. Further bodies come after this core, as discussed below, but all are related to it.

The original FATF 40 Recommendations were steadily being implemented into local laws until the attack on the World Trade Center on 11 September 2001 (9/11) when terrorists flew aeroplanes into the twin towers in New York. These 9/11 atrocities, which claimed the lives of over 3,000 people, sparked an urgent desire by governments to stop terrorist groups from using their financial systems to gather the funds required to carry out terrorist acts, and Counter-Terrorist Financing (CTF) activity began in earnest. Members of FATF, again recognizing that a coordinated international approach was the way forward, introduced its Nine Special Recommendations for this purpose. The added impetus caused by 9/11 also fuelled the drive for global inclusion, and more countries, some of those considered higher risk by Transparency International, themselves enacted AML and CTF laws, all based on FATF's international standard Recommendations.

This international and coordinated approach to implementing controls for AML and CTF is good news for organizations and AML professionals alike. Wherever we are in the world the core principles are well established and accepted by the international community: they apply to all of us. The FATF 40 Recommendations and Nine Special Recommendations introduced after the 9/11 attack on the New York World Trade Center were consolidated back into 40 core Recommendations in 2012. The Recommendations are listed in Table 1.1.

Who are the players?

The Egmont Group of Financial Intelligence Units

The Egmont Group of FIUs (Egmont Group) was established in 1995, with members consisting of government law-making bodies collaborating together. The Egmont Group identified the United Nations Convention Against Illicit Traffic in Narcotic Drugs and

Table 1.1 Summary of the Financial Action Task Force Recommendations

International standards on combating money laundering and the financing of terrorism and proliferation			
Section		**No**	**Recommendation**
A	Anti-money laundering/ counter-terrorist financing policies and coordination	1	Assessing risks and applying a risk-based approach
		2	National cooperation and coordination
B	Money laundering and confiscation	3	Money laundering offence
		4	Confiscation and provisional measures
C	Terrorist financing and financing of proliferation	5	Terrorist financing offence
		6	Targeted financial sanctions related to terrorism and terrorist financing
		7	Targeted financial sanctions related to proliferation
		8	Non-profit organizations
D	Preventive measures	9	Financial institution secrecy laws
		10	Customer due diligence
		11	Record keeping
		12	Politically exposed persons
		13	Correspondent banking
		14	Money or value transfer services
		15	New technologies
		16	Wire transfers
		17	Reliance on third parties
		18	Internal controls and foreign branches and subsidiaries
		19	Higher-risk countries
		20	Reporting of suspicious transactions
		21	Tipping-off and confidentiality
		22	Designated non-financial businesses and professions (DNFBPs): Customer due diligence
		23	DNFBPs: Other measures
E	Transparency and beneficial ownership of legal persons and arrangements	24	Transparency and beneficial ownership of legal persons
		25	Transparency and beneficial ownership of legal arrangements

(*continued*)

Table 1.1 *(Continued)*

International standards on combating money laundering and the financing of terrorism and proliferation			
Section		**No**	**Recommendation**
F	Powers and responsibilities of competent authorities and other institutional measures	26	Regulation and supervision of financial institutions
		27	Powers of supervisors
		28	Regulation and supervision of DNFBPs
		29	Financial intelligence units
		30	Responsibilities of law enforcement and investigative authorities
		31	Powers of law enforcement and investigative authorities
		32	Cash couriers
		33	Statistics
		34	Guidance and feedback
		35	Sanctions
G	International cooperation	36	International instruments
		37	Mutual legal assistance
		38	Mutual legal assistance: freezing and confiscation
		39	Extradition
		40	Other forms of international cooperation

These recommendations were adopted by FATF on 15 February 2012

Psychotropic Substances (1988) as the start of a trend towards establishing an international strategy for anti-money laundering, and its focus is to address the questions: 'What structures do nations need in place to enable them to investigate instances of money laundering, how will they be funded, and what will their responsibilities be?'

Establishment of the Egmont Group was timely, as in 1994 the first online bank account was launched in the United States by the Stanford Credit Union, and by 2001, eight US banks reported having over 1 million online customers each. By 2012, the US Online Banking Report claimed that 33 million people globally banked online, including via mobile phones (Bruene, 2012). This innovation brought a very useful new vehicle for the laundering of money, and progress in controlling transactions in this area became a critical element in fighting organized crime and drug trafficking by interrupting the flow of funds.

As Egmont Group members started to develop their AML strategies, they found that their local laws did not give sufficient access to the financial information they needed, and they did not have the engagement of financial services organizations. They needed engagement with financial services and the introduction of systems and controls to foster transparency and accountability to help control the flow of laundered money, together with reporting of suspicious transactions to the FIUs.

The Wolfsberg Group

International interest in reducing the use of banks as laundering vehicles led to the formation of industry body, the Wolfsberg Group, in 2000. The Wolfsberg Group is a non-governmental organization (NGO) with an interest in providing clear guidance to banks in all jurisdictions to reduce their exposure to money laundering risk by following principles set on its website (see the end of this chapter). This consolidated approach across nations gives clear indication to new banks, developing nations and AML professionals when strengthening organizational controls as to what they can do on a practical basis. The principles are not binding, and notable Wolfsberg members such as HSBC, which gave input to their creation and knew the purpose of their formation, move away from them on occasion to their detriment, as discussed in Case Study 8.2. Another NGO, Transparency International (TI) assisted the formation and launch of the Wolfsberg Group with the intention of reducing the reputational damage inflicted by money laundering scandals in the banking sector.

Transparency International

Germany-based TI was formed in 1993 to raise public awareness of corruption when exporting nations pay bribes to government officials and political players in developing nations in what they call arrangements of 'grand corruption'. TI has successfully brought together alliances of businesses and governmental bodies in close to 100 nations to reduce the risk of bribery of government officials, which is very much in support of the US Foreign Corrupt Practices Act 1977 (FCPA). When carrying out a money laundering risk assessment on entering a new market, the TI corruption perceptions index is a useful tool, which can be found on its website (see the end of this chapter). Updated each year, around 170 jurisdictions are ranked on perception of the risks they pose to businesses, and the countries move up and down the list: countries that improve their money laundering and other legislation to control risks tend to move up the list (ranking 1 being the country perceived as being least risky) taking the places of those that do not. The list is a practical guide to any organization seeking to minimize its risk in the pursuance of its activities. AML professionals use it to allocate risk levels and appropriate controls to branches and subsidiaries on a country basis. (There is more about country risk in Chapter 5.)

United Nations Office on Drugs and Crime (UNODC)

UNODC was established in 1997 with the purpose of helping countries to draft and implement local legislation giving effect to international treaties including the initiatives of AML groups such as FATF. This is very useful to countries seeking to implement relevant AML laws as UNODC, via its Global Programme Against Money Laundering (GPML) produced the UNODC Model Money Laundering, Proceeds of Crime and Terrorist Financing Bill 2003, a model law that countries can use as an AML programme template. It also encourages cross-border AML activity coordination, the development of AML policy and raising money laundering awareness, which you may find useful in the AML risk assessment of your organization.

Stop and think

Which AML bodies are active in your region? Register for online AML regulatory updates to keep pace with local relevant developments. See the end of the chapter for the addresses of some notable websites.

European AML Directives

As the international initiatives giving soft law best practices and recommendations began to be underpinned by legislation, the first European Union Directive on the Prevention of the Use of the Financial System for the Purposes of Money Laundering (91/308/EEC) was introduced in 1991. This initiative is a microcosm of international cooperation in AML, and the EU AML Directives give a logical flow of development as to how it is that your organization is now an obliged entity, or may become one in the future.

The Directive, known as 1MLD, was narrow in its focus in line with the thinking of the day. It covered only financial institutions and the proceeds of drug trafficking, and it introduced money laundering as a criminal activity. It imposed a number of requirements on the financial institutions of EU Member States, including the need to verify the identity of customers and keep appropriate records, implement systems and controls to prevent the institution from being used to launder the proceeds of drug trafficking, and report suspicious transactions to the local FIU. 1MLD introduced the requirement for employee training and awareness of money laundering, giving them the knowledge of what money laundering behaviour looks like while not letting the criminal know that they are aware of their activities, or 'tipping them off' to the fact that they are under suspicion. (See Chapter 7 for more on tipping off.)

In 2001 the Second European Union Anti-Money Laundering Directive (2MLD) came into force, the effect of which was to extend the reach of money laundering legislation beyond financial institutions and into the realm of professional advisers, such as tax advisers and the legal and accountancy professions. Gatekeepers such as these can allow financial arrangements to be made that infect seemingly legitimate arrangements with criminal funds. 2MLD moved the focus of attention to them, closing the door to criminals wishing to benefit from their advice on the way to laundering their funds. Transactions in high-value goods were also included, bringing dealers of artworks, precious metals and stones into the regulated sector, along with auctioneers and casinos. The sale and purchase of real estate both for business and personal housing use became regulated activities.

Following this the Third European Union Anti-Money Laundering Directive (3MLD) implemented the revisions to the June 2003 FATF 40 Recommendations, plus the Nine Special Recommendations on terrorism. Whereas under 2MLD client identification and verification were known as Know Your Customer (KYC), under 3MLD the four aspects to client checking are clarified and renamed as Client Due Diligence (CDD). CDD is expanded from the requirement to identify and verify customer identity, to identifying all 'beneficial owners' (a natural person who has an interest in any relevant property of 25 per cent or more). 3MLD requires regulated entities to obtain information on the purpose and intended nature of the business relationship between entity and customer, and ongoing monitoring of the business relationship.

CDD is applied using a risk-based approach. Under 3MLD obliged entities can carry out simplified due diligence (SDD) for low-risk products, entities, geographies or individuals. Enhanced due diligence (EDD) is required for high-risk situations, for example where the person in question is a foreign politically exposed person (PEP). Carrying out due diligence is where anomalies can be found and 'red flags' are raised, ie any activity that appears to be outside the norm for the customer. An example would be an organization stating at the outset that its business is wholly carried out in Europe, and then taking payments in from Nigeria. 3MLD requires regulated entities to understand their client relationship and the source of their funds. The requirements on organizations and their AML professionals became more onerous and sophisticated to prevent money launderers from gaining access to their systems. (CDD is discussed in more detail in Chapter 4.)

Moving forward a decade, and the Fourth European Union Anti-Money Laundering Directive (4MLD) placed a greater emphasis on the risk-based approach of due diligence. For example, any countries outside of the EU, 'third countries', are deemed to be higher risk by the European Commission, and subject to EDD. Risk assessments as required by 4MLD are there to ensure that obliged entities in EU Member States clearly understand the money laundering and terrorist financing risks that affect them. 4MLD is a minimum Harmonizing Directive, which means that EU member states can adopt stricter regulations than required by it, should they wish.

In 4MLD, the regulatory scope is extended to gambling services rather than casinos only. The threshold over which persons accepting cash payments for goods have to conduct CDD reduced to €10,000. CDD itself becomes more interesting, as 4MLD removes the ability of organizations to exempt pooled accounts and listed companies from their checking activities, and it provides further freedom for organizations to justify how they have used their risk assessment to apply a particular level of due diligence to a client. Because of this, Customer Risk Assessments (CRAs) are destined to play a larger role in regulatory oversight activity, and warrant the particular attention of AML professionals.

Under 4MLD the definition of PEPs, individuals entrusted with prominent public functions, is expanded to include domestic PEPs for the first time. Their position and influence give them potential opportunities to receive bribes and money that may be laundered following various predicate offences.

In line with the trend of increased responsibility for senior management, under 4MLD senior executives are held responsible for the approval of AML policies, controls and procedures, together with their monitoring and enhancement over time, and the level of financial penalties for violations of the Directive are increased. 4MLD also re-aligns SDD and EDD. No blanket exemptions are allowed for pooled accounts, listed or other regulated entities. In assessing risk elements, customer risk, product, service transaction or delivery channel risk and geographical risk are all factors, and the European Supervisory Authority (ESA) Risk Factor Guidelines 2017 assist organizations in assessing the level of due diligence required. They place the CDD of obliged entities central to this process for both risk assessment and risk management purposes. The document reiterates the meaning of CDD from Article 13(1) of 4MLD as:

- identifying the customer and verifying the customer's identity on the basis of documents, data or information obtained from a reliable and independent source;
- identifying the customer's beneficial owner and taking reasonable measures to verify their identity so that the obliged entity is satisfied that it knows who the beneficial owner is;

- assessing and, as appropriate, obtaining information on the purpose and intended nature of the business relationship, and
- conducting ongoing monitoring of the business relationship. This includes transaction monitoring and keeping the underlying information up to date. (Joint Committee of the European Supervisory Authorities, 2017)

(Chapter 3 provides more information on identification and management of risk, using the AML strategy wheel.)

4MLD sets out comprehensive requirements that spring from FATF guidelines agreed in 2012, and its content is relevant as a benchmark for organizations across the globe when implementing AML and counter-terrorist financing controls. Under 4MLD there are noteworthy exemptions from scope, which helps to limit the number of obliged entities where risk is low:

- *Gambling services (not casinos):* new exemption, not available under 3MLD; exemption available where risk is assessed as low; gambling services exemptions must be notified to the European Commission.
- *Financial activity where limited:* limited in turnover, below the threshold set at national level; limited number of transactions, singly or aggregated, too low to facilitate money laundering with maximum value of €1,000; financial activity is not the organization's main activity, where the main activity is not caught under 4MLD and the financial activity is only provided to customers of the main activity of the organization.

When 4MLD came into force in June 2015, with a national transposition deadline of June 2017, one might have reasonably expected there would be another gap in regulatory change to enable its requirements to be implemented and tested. However, amending legislative proposals were published in July 2016 for the Fifth European Union Anti-Money Laundering Directive (5MLD). With AML and CTF high on political agendas around the world in the light of terrorist activity, these proposals came hot on the heels of 4MLD. All of this activity is to align the EU with current FATF guidelines, a key part of which is to adopt a risk-based approach to the implementation of appropriate strategies to mitigate AML organizational risks. To provide clarity for organizations when implementing controls required by 4MLD, a summary of the key changes for financial services firms and obliged entities can be found in Chapter 4.

Under 5MLD the scope of obliged entities extends further, to virtual currency exchange platforms and custodian wallet providers. Its two main objectives are to strengthen transparency rules to prevent large-scale concealment of funds, and to further close down the financial means of criminals without preventing the functioning of markets and payment systems. In addition to enhancing the powers of FIUs in the EU and giving better public access to beneficial ownership registers, 5MLD has a focus on electronic payments, reducing the threshold for identifying holders of prepaid cards from €250 to €150, and requiring virtual currency exchange platforms and custodian wallet providers to carry out customer due diligence.

Immense changes in money laundering regulation can be seen in the iterations of the EU money laundering Directives. This is unlikely to slow down, and it requires that AML professionals are diligent in keeping up to date with developments and the application of new measures to keep their organizations compliant.

Stop and think

Is your organization keeping pace with AML regulatory change? Check when the AML controls in your organization were introduced or last revised.

United Kingdom Economic Crime Offence and the Criminal Finances Act 2017

In the UK, the Criminal Finances Act 2017 (CFA) introduced the most significant changes to its AML regime in a decade. The CFA acknowledges the attractive nature of the UK financial and professional services sector, its open economy and the high-end property market of the capital city as a magnet to money launderers. The CFA introduces new powers of disclosure and unexplained wealth orders to assist law enforcement in gaining the information it needs to prove a case. Under prior UK legislation, disclosure orders were not possible for money laundering investigations. Also, access to information was limited to that requested in a court order. Before the CFA, several court orders may have been required as an AML investigation progressed. With the new process in place the disclosure order is in force for the length of the investigation and it can be used in money laundering investigations. These disclosures will be applicable to any person, not just to those in financial services, considered to have information relevant to the investigation.

The CFA also introduces Unexplained Wealth Orders. These require a person or a company to explain the origin of their wealth if their assets appear to be disproportionate to their taxed income, but only if they are also suspected of having association with criminal activity. For overseas criminals laundering money by purchases on the London property market, should they fail to respond to the Unexplained Wealth Order and justify their purchase, the property could be seized by law enforcement agencies.

This move to introduce an economic crime offence in the UK gathered pace with a call for evidence from the Ministry of Justice during January to March 2017 to better restrict the bad practices and governance allowed by gaps in existing UK legislation, including tax evasion that leads to money laundering. The CFA addresses difficulties in criminally prosecuting larger organizations, which can lead to the prosecution of smaller organizations and individual employees rather than their employers, as the 'directing mind and will' test used in prosecutions is easier to apply. The economic crime offence has the effect of placing governance responsibility in the hands of senior management, similar to that of obliged organizations, with the aim of:

- Having boards and senior managers ask the questions to disclose bad practices rather than leaving them to the business areas and claiming no knowledge.
- Ensuring that meeting minutes and the recording of attendees and matters discussed are subject to senior management sign-off.

- Requiring electronic communications to occur using authorized addresses and channels, including e-mail, rather than allowing the use of personal e-mail accounts to avoid leaving an audit trail. This element was a significant factor in the United States election campaign in late 2016, when Hilary Clinton was accused of misuse of a personal e-mail account to hide communications (Graff, 2016).
- Ceasing the practice of not disturbing senior management by implementing corporate structures that allow significant decisions to be made further down the organization to insulate senior management and the board from malpractice.
- Preventing the use of zero asset companies to negotiate with third-party agents on behalf of the organization.

In this, as in other UK laws, notably the UK Bribery Act 2010, failure to prevent can form an element of the offence. Is this the shape of AML regulation to come? Cases brought under the CFA would have to prove that the offence occurred as a result of the company's processes, procedures and other control failures to prevent criminal activity from occurring. Are the AML controls in place for your UK headquartered organization robust enough to withstand enquiry under this law? It may be a good time to analyse any risk exposures and carry out a review!

The groups, directives, laws and regulations discussed in this chapter plot the course of the international efforts to disrupt the flow of criminal money passing across borders and make it harder for criminals to enjoy the wealth gained from their activities. As more countries strive to provide regulatory structures to prevent money laundering, the drive to trade on the international stage powerfully draws more countries into compliance with the FATF 40 Recommendations around the globe. Good news for AML professionals!

Key takeaways

- The OECD nations created FATF in 1989 to combat the money laundering of drug traffickers seeking to clean their criminal money by taking it across borders into new jurisdictions.

- AML Mission Central is the FATF: the 40 Recommendations have defined money laundering controls globally since 1989 and FATF is instrumental today in pushing forward the AML agenda.
- Regulatory development is reactive to the new threats of money laundering, and after the 9/11 atrocity, CTF Recommendations were added to the original 40. These were all summarized back to 40 Recommendations in 2012.
- Money laundering can follow the traditional placement, layering, integration model of moving funds derived from a predicate crime through the financial services system to produce 'clean' money. However, money laundering does not need a cash element. It can also be the benefit from any proceeds of crime, including high-value goods, without money ever changing hands.
- There is a movement towards making organizations responsible for preventing some types of financial crime such as bribery and corruption, and tax evasion. New laws are being enacted that require 'adequate' or 'reasonable' procedures to be in place to prevent criminal activity. AML professionals should be aware of 'failure to prevent' requirements affecting their organization.
- Countries are gradually implementing the FATF recommendations into local law, encouraged by the mutual evaluation programme.
- Observing AML legal and regulatory change, such as the EU's 4MLD, helps countries globally to keep up to date with current AML and CTF expectations.
- AML obligations continue to reach out beyond financial services, to better prevent organizations from being used to launder the proceeds of crime.

Notable websites

Egmont Group: www.egmontgroup.org

Financial Action Task Force: www.fatf-gafi.org

Organisation for Economic Cooperation and Development: http://www.oecd.org

Organised Crime and Corruption Reporting Project: https://www.occrp.org

Transparency International: https://www.transparency.org

United Nations Convention Against Illicit Traffic in Narcotic Drugs and Psychotropic Substances (1998): https://www.unodc.org/pdf/convention_1988_en.pdf

United Nations Office on Drugs and Crime: www.unodc.org

Wolfsberg Group: http://www.wolfsberg-principles.com

www.coe.int/en/web/moneyval/activities/typologies

References and further reading

Batchelor, T (2017) Keith Palmer: Policeman stabbed to death in London terror attack named (22/3), available from: http://www.independent.co.uk/news/uk/home-news/keith-palmer-policeman-stabbing-death-named-london-terror-attack-westminster-a7644811.html (last accessed 30 January 2018)

Bruene, J (2012) Online & Mobile Banking Forecast: Current, Future and historical Usage: 1994 to 2021, available from: https://www.digitalbankingreport.com/dbr/obr200/ (last accessed 30 January 2018)

CNN (2016) US Airport Theft Investigation, 07/04, available from: http://edition.cnn.com/2016/04/07/us/airport-theft-investigation/index.html (last accessed 8 October 2017)

FATF (2012–2017), International Standards on Combating Money Laundering and the Financing of Terrorism & Proliferation, FATF, Paris, available from: www.fatf-gafi.org/recommendations.html (last accessed 30 January 2018)

Financial Conduct Authority (2012) Final Notice Coutts & Company 23 March 2012, available from: www.fca.org.uk/publication/final-notices/coutts-mar12.pdf (last accessed 24 January 2018)

Graff, G M (2016) What the FBI Files Reveal About Hillary Clinton's Email Server, 30/9, available from: www.politico.com/magazine/story/2016/09/hillary-clinton-emails-2016-server-state-department-fbi-214307 (last accessed 24 January 2018)

International Monetary Fund (2004) Financial intelligence units: an overview, available from: https:www.imf.org/external/pubs/ft/FIU/fiu.pdf (last accessed 24 January 2018)

Joint Committee of the European Supervisory Authorities (2017) Final Guidelines: Joint Guidelines under Articles 17 and 18(4) of Directive (EU) 2015/849 on simplified and enhanced customer due diligence and the factors credit and financial institutions should consider when assessing the money laundering and terrorist financing risk associated with individual business relationships and occasional transactions: The Risk Factor Guidelines, available at: www.eba.europa.eu/documents/10180/1890686/Final+Guidelines+on+Risk+Factors+%28JC+2017+37%29.pdf (last accessed 24 January 2018)

The Money Laundering, Terrorist Financing and Transfer of Funds (Information on the Payer) Regulations 2017 (SI 692), available at: www.legislation.gov.uk/uksi/2017/692/pdfs/uksi_20170692_en.pdf (last accessed 24 January 2018)

MONEYVAL (2012) 6 Research Report: Criminal money flows on the Internet: methods, trends and multi-stakeholder counteraction, available from: https://rm.coe.int/research-report-criminal-money-flows-on-the-internet-methods-trends-an/168071509a (last accessed 6 February 2018)

OCCRP (2017) The Russian Laundromat Exposed, 20/03, available from: www.occrp.org/en/laundromat/the-russian-laundromat-exposed (last accessed 24 January 2018)

Rapport, M (2004) Stanford FCU Set to Mark 10-Year Anniversary as First Financial to Offer Online Banking, 4/2, available from: http://www.cutimes.com/2004/02/04/stanford-fcu-set-to-mark-10year-anniversary-as-first-financial-to-offer-online-banking (last accessed 30 January 2018)

SEC v Kenneth L Lay, Jeffrey K Skilling, Richard A Causey (2004) Civil Action No. H-04-0284 (Harmon), available from: https://www.sec.gov/litigation/complaints/comp18776.pdf (last accessed 30 January 2018)

Implementing an anti-money laundering risk control framework 02

This chapter covers:

- Strategy and the link to risk appetite.
- Governance and AML control environment.
- Maximizing benefit to the business.
- Employee management: role profiles.
- AML training plan.
- Performance management.
- Employee communications
- Gaps and overlaps.

Strategy and the link to risk appetite

Broadly speaking the strategy of an organization will establish its risk appetite, which will then guide its governance and control environment, providing the ethos of the organization and expressing its culture and values. The mere expression of value statements by company Chief Executive Officers (CEOs) does not, of course, itself guide organizations; it is the control environment that is created and maintained to support the value statements that give them their existence in reality. Business strategy that is developed by the guiding minds of the organization will contain its unique risk elements. Their analysis gives a starting point from which to establish the control environment and governance required to run the organization in compliance with laws and regulations, including AML. Organizations grow and develop as opportunities (as well as challenges) present themselves, and it is likely that the governance and control environment will have to grow with the organization, so you as the AML professional will have to bear this in mind when developing your financial crime and AML policies.

Governance and AML control environment

Having established the strategy and risk appetite, the next step in developing a governance and control environment will provide structure and parameters within which to work. Care taken to balance commercial risk with regulatory compliance in establishing controls is a key element in ensuring their effectiveness. This is because effectiveness is either improved or diminished by the way new controls are received by employees. If employees can see the controls are proportionate and necessary, and maybe even help their work, they are more likely to be supportive, which is important as the success of the control environment depends in part on the way employees react to it. AML professionals are looking for a successful implementation to improve the culture of the organization, and this resides within its workforce.

Whereas policies may be written to comply with all relevant laws and regulations, the organization's risk appetite and strategy will encourage employee attitude either towards or away from the policies as written. In organizations that give 'lip service' to the things they know they have to do by law, but the guiding minds of the company make decisions according to their risk appetite rather than in accordance with the policies, governance is undermined. The AML compliance programme will suffer as a result, and leave the organization open to being used for money laundering.

Maximizing benefit to the business

Collaboration between governance functions in creating an employee code of conduct, including Human Resources (HR) as well as Compliance and Legal, is a facet of policy writing that can improve practical application in the business. Time spent with business areas when writing policies will also greatly improve their practical application, as resource within the business area will truly understand what is in the policy and why it is there. The best policies we have seen support activity carried out in the business and have gained the active support of management and employees alike. Where companies buy in ready-made policies from external providers who have little knowledge of the organization, they may make those statements required by law thoroughly and in legalese to cover the statutory requirements, but have little usefulness or application within the organization and so fail to provide guidance to control employee behaviour. Where 'off the shelf' policies are bought in it is unlikely that procedures will align well with them, and employee respect of and adherence to them will be impaired.

Employee management

Effective employee management starts with the first encounter of the prospective employee with the organization. When hiring employees, including AML team members, well written role profiles help to underpin the control of employee behaviour from the beginning, and where they are lacking or unclear, effective employee management can be difficult to achieve. Although there has to be room in the role profile for changing expectations as time progresses, clarity of expectation from the start gives both employee and manager the role activities for measuring at annual appraisals without unwelcome surprises, and they will form part of activity mapping against the plan for AML risk management.

In AML compliance planning, the role profiles are useful as a gap analysis in risk profiling the activities of the department itself. Your AML personnel, working efficiently, must be able to cover all of the

Table 2.1 Role profile mapping

Role profile	Element	Purpose
Role title	Have the role title consistent with the employee grade/ level within the organization.	Consistency of titles allows for a 'shorthand' of nomenclature to develop, giving immediate indication of seniority and purpose of the role. When issuing online training, online categories can then be chosen for, or excluded from, the training without the need for manual intervention of employee lists.
Department/ Section	Both elements together are desirable to ensure clarity of targeting of training.	As above, it is possible to minimize the amount of administrative time spent on creating groups of trainees, if instead of using employee names, which are always subject to change with new hires, leavers and movers with the organization, the department and section form part of the essential HR record of the role.
Reporting to	Immediate supervising manager recorded, without any dual or 'dotted line' reporting.	Clarity of reporting lines helps to fix responsibility of activities, making the control environment more transparent, and helping to prevent gaps and overlaps, which employees with criminal intent might exploit to use the organization for their money laundering activities.
Direct reports/Team	A record of all team members reporting into the employee.	Updating of these records on the HR system in a timely manner makes the difference of rolling out training to all of the right people at the right time. Where HR records are allowed to remain out of date, the very employees who may come into contact with potential money laundering customers may be missed off the training list. This sort of professional negligence is a prime indicator of the attention given to money laundering prevention in the organization by regulatory bodies.

(continued)

Table 2.1 *(Continued)*

Role profile	Element	Purpose
Main purposes of the role	Clarity of purpose of the role, breaking down different facets, and including the inevitable catch-all of 'and other duties relevant to the role' to allow for changes within the organization.	Clarity is essential to the main purposes of an AML compliance role, at any level of team membership and management. It should be written to inform the key results/outcomes of the role to form part of the jigsaw of roles within AML compliance in the organization. The role purpose should also give an indication of both the internal and external liaison necessary to engage effectively with business areas, governance stakeholders and external parties.
Main tasks	Tasks, the completion of which support the purpose of the role.	Tasks provide direction to employees as to the bulk of their work. Using directional terms such as 'initiate' and 'complete', the description of the task helps both the employee and manager at appraisal time assess whether the employee is fulfilling the purpose of the role.
Key results/ outcomes	The things a successful incumbent will achieve.	As above, the key results and outcomes give a clear indication of what good looks like, and the AML risks mitigated by having an effective employee in the role.

duties required by the AML governance plan, including those activities supported by software systems. You may find it helpful to use the mapping tool in Table 2.1 to assist in building role profiles, which is as effective in designing roles for AML professionals as it is for roles in other parts of the organization.

AML risk assessment in role profiling compliance team members, in the knowledge of what the organization's strategy, industry and attendant risks are, may fall to the AML compliance officer. However, the HR department may already have mapped out high-level roles and responsibilities for the organization, and collaboration with them may effectively align the AML team closer to the organization's workforce matrix than is possible by working alone.

1 AML compliance training

Once the new hire is in role, AML compliance training can start. As a general introduction, where the training is standard for all new hires, the AML element can effectively form part of anti-bribery and corruption (ABC) training, or financial crime training. It could usefully begin with positioning information on the state of AML laws and regulation today via the development of the Financial Action Task Force's (FATF's) 40 Recommendations and the international collaborative organizations such as the Egmont group, discussed in Chapter 1, as well as the early focus of AML activity being almost exclusively the prevention of the proceeds of drug trafficking across national boundaries. Following this with the strengthening of financial services regulation to prevent terrorist financing and more recently the expansion of AML-obliged organizations to include the legal and accounting professions, real estate, company service providers and gambling, and introducing the controls you have in place because of them, will bring the new hire right up to date with current money laundering prevention activity in your organization.

In many jurisdictions, the role of Money Laundering Reporting Officer (MLRO) or equivalent, includes the requirement to train employees adequately. In the UK, there is currently no requirement for MLROs to have any specific qualification or proof of competence, nor any requirement for the organization to provide them with training to become competent before accepting the role. Once in the role, however, there is the requirement for MLROs to provide training to employees, and their failure to adequately provide this may result in regulatory sanctions, including fines and removal from the role.

Training is, therefore, a high priority for MLROs, and in particular proof of employee competence after the training has taken place, bringing a focus of testing into the arena. Gone are the days when giving a face-to-face presentation to employees whose responsibilities included AML-type activity was enough to prove that training had been given and received. Trainees could claim the training was boring or uninteresting so they didn't listen and just devoured the coffee and biscuits as a diversion, rendering the training ineffective in the eyes of scrutineers.

So, when providing AML training to your organization, think more of training for competence rather than providing training for information needs. The AML competence of all relevant employees is an essential control on which the MLRO can rely. Periodic refresher training maintains that competence and does not let it lapse. The role of the AML Training Officer within the team is a key de-risking element for both the MLRO and the organization, and maintaining auditable records of training given and received, including whether the trainee passed or failed the accompanying tests, is essential to provide evidence of the requirement fulfilled. An AML training plan could look like this:

Onboarding

Method: Face-to-face or online company-specific training.

Audience: Colleagues (employees and contractors) new to the organization.

Purpose: Orientation, for all new hires, general in nature.

Test? Questions and activities but no test.

Development

Method: Externally provided, including certification.

Audience: Employees with key roles and responsibilities forming the backbone of the AML team.

Purpose: Provide high-performing employees with qualifications to enable them to understand the regulatory environment in which they operate.

Test? Yes.

Role-specific

Method: Face-to-face or online company-specific training, sourced internally or with external support.

Audience: Colleagues in each essential AML role and activity.

Purpose: Provide colleagues with direction for their work, including rationale as to why it is important.

Test? Yes.

Senior management

Method: Face-to-face or online company-specific training, sourced internally or with external support.

Audience: All members of the senior management team, regardless of role.

Purpose: Ensure that senior management are kept fully up to date with developments in AML regulatory requirements, and their involvement.

Test? Unlikely.

AML topic periodic reminders

Method: E-mail, intranet banner or news item.

Audience: All colleagues.

Purpose: Keep AML compliance front of mind. Useful as one in a series of compliance-related regular updates.

Test? No.

Code of business conduct and certification to policies, including AML

Method: Online preferred.

Audience: All colleagues, including senior management, the board – everyone.

Purpose: Provide the entire organization with the same governance structure and ensure they know it means them.

Test? Yes.

Regulator seminars

Method: Seminars provided at central external venue.

Audience: Relevant employees.

Purpose: Demonstrate engagement with the AML regulator. Some keep registers, using these to help risk-profile organizations.

Test? No.

Training is not only essential for AML compliance professionals to know how to do their job properly, it also educates the entire organization in what financial crime and money laundering look like. Colleagues will be better able to raise red flags to activities internal to the organization even if they are not directly situated in AML compliance. The first step is to gain agreement from other governance functions that training is necessary to achieve compliance. In a decentralized organization, it is easy for remote branches to think they are out of sight and so beyond the reach of head office. Encouraged to consider their authority as the highest locally, some can be tempted into wrongdoing. Providing training and reminders of a reporting mechanism to employees in-country can alert all to the behaviours expected of them; this was Saskia's aim in Case Study 2.1 in providing guidance to senior account managers.

CASE STUDY 2.1: Providing guidance to senior account managers

In London, Saskia, a financial services industry AML compliance professional, was drafted in to an organization whose company service activities were about to be included in the AML regulatory sphere. Surveying the horizon risks of the organization against its multinational structure, Saskia could see that in a year or two the organization would need to truly understand its AML risks and have a control framework in place to manage them.

Along with her AML duties, Saskia was a member of the internal investigations team and she noticed a number of Code of Conduct breaches by senior account managers in several jurisdictions, which varied from fraudulent business arrangements by misuse of company assets and services for personal gain, to manipulation of procurement systems to award themselves consultancy fees paid to shell companies. Very creative misuse, but why did the account managers think they could do these things? The organization had a decentralized management style where the separate countries were responsible for all of their local compliance activities, and the most successful members of their sales team were promoted into the role of senior account manager for the country. Being decentralized, the account managers knew that as long as the numbers looked good and there were no surprises, they were left to run the local branch undisturbed. On promoting the account managers to their senior role, the organization depended on their business and local knowledge to inform them of their duties and did not think it necessary to provide them with any training.

Although it would have been easier for Saskia to consider the senior account managers as bad people, she took the view that good people can become bad when temptation is placed before them, and set about lobbying to provide financial crime risk training to relevant employees in the sales team, together with their support functions of Company Secretariat, HR and Finance. Although HR and Finance did have some resources around the world, Company Secretariat was based only in the UK, so Saskia first approached Company Secretariat to see if they would like to collaborate with AML Compliance on creating some training for the senior account managers. Using a directors' duties training storyboard, Saskia adapted it to raise specific Code of Conduct policy requirements, including gifts and entertainment, conflicts of interest, together with awareness of the whistleblowing hotline, reiterating the requirement on each employee to report Code of Conduct breaches.

Questions

1. Does your organization have a centralized or decentralized business model? Centralized is where control is kept centrally over AML and other regulatory controls, and decentralized is where control is kept locally, without direction from head office.
2. On what criteria are in-country senior managers promoted in your organization? Are they successful sales people, entrusted to grow the business?
3. What training do they receive upon appointment?
4. With whom in your organization would you need to collaborate to produce effective in-country training to senior account managers?
5. How could you deliver the training? Would online training or face-to-face work best for your organization?

In the same way as the international standard-setting bodies offer best practice in AML controls, training that offers international best practice guidance on their implementation, such as that provided by the International Compliance Association, gives assurance to the organizations and students taking their courses and examinations that the content is relevant to controlling financial crime and AML risks in organizations across the globe. Such training and certification give a strong boost to the CV of trainees, making them more employable both locally and internationally at all levels of seniority. Training is also a good defence for an organization when employees go rogue, such as in Case Study 2.2, Morgan Stanley (US v Peterson).

CASE STUDY 2.2: Morgan Stanley

A former managing director of Morgan Stanley's real estate business in China, Garth Peterson, breached the US Foreign Corrupt Practices Act (FCPA) by bribing a government official in order to grow the business. Fortunately for Morgan Stanley, to manage its global business effectively the organization had protected itself with policies and procedures. Regular communications and training were also provided extensively to employees in the jurisdictions in which it operated.

An organization can never completely eradicate the risk of employees turning to crime and attempting to use its facilities to commit fraud or money laundering, but in the case of Garth Peterson, Morgan Stanley was able to prove that it provided him with training on the FCPA seven times over the six years in question, 2002 to 2008; in addition he received no less than 35 FCPA compliance reminders. Morgan Stanley also required Garth Peterson to certify to its policies numerous times and kept this on his permanent employment record, with annual certification of policies being standard practice.

In view of its extensive financial crime prevention programme, in 2012 the US Department of Justice (DoJ) decided not to prosecute Morgan Stanley. This was a triumph of corporate compliance activity, to de-risk the organization to the extent that it could defend itself from prosecution by virtue of a robust compliance programme, protecting the organization from censure. Garth Peterson suffered a $250,000 fine, the loss of $3 million laundered money in real estate in China, and a nine-month prison sentence. Once the DoJ had finished with the case, it passed its information over to the Chinese authorities. The information included evidence of bribes given by Garth Peterson to a Chinese government official who held the position of Chairman of Yonge Enterprise (Group) Co Ltd (Yonge), which was a large real estate development arm of the Luwan District Government in Shanghai. The Chinese authorities then investigated the case, found the Chairman of Yonge guilty, and sentenced him to death.

Questions

1. Who is responsible for sending out employee communications in your organization?
2. Does your organization have a calendar of regulatory reminder communications to employees?

3 Whose responsibility is it to write AML reminder communications?

4 Who approves them for publication?

5 Do you have auditable records of the AML communications sent that are sufficient to provide a defence for your organization should they be called for?

When considering Case Study 2.2 it is scary to think that the full force of the law may apply when a political regime moves from 'zero to hero' in terms of its attention to the controls necessary to participate in trade on an international scale. The essential nature of embedding international soft law conventions, in this case best practice guidelines offered by the Organization for Economic Co-operation and Development (OECD), into the corporate governance of the organization has a de-risking effect. Here, it worked across continental divides of culture in Morgan Stanley, clearly expressing via training and regular reminders the expected behaviour of employees. In the United States the OECD guidelines, although not binding upon member jurisdictions, have been embedded into the guidelines for legal action, the US Sentencing Guidelines (United States Sentencing Commission, 2016) where their effective application offers protection against prosecution. Morgan Stanley was protected by having evidence of good governance controls in place, which acted as an effective defence:

> Recognizing that a compliance program is not available as a formal affirmative defense, it is clear that Morgan Stanley was able to use not only their written compliance program but its ongoing maintenance, communication and due diligence aspects to shield the employer from liability. (Fox, 2012)

2 Performance management

The next item on the agenda for de-risking the organization is performance management, and this starts with goal setting. Where goal setting provides high-level, broad expectations, such as 'provide support to the AML compliance function', they are not specific enough to provide clarity for the team activity gap analysis, nor for performance management in the case of failing employees. The more specific variety of goal setting ideally lists the areas of responsibility from the employee role description, with further detail where necessary. In turn, this can prove helpful in managing underperforming employees as the consistency of approach gives no surprises, and avoids claims by employees that the activity they are being judged as lacking in does not form part of their role. Specifics take longer to establish than generalities, of course, and the balance of granularity with a quicker, broader view is one to be discussed with the HR team when assessing performance management, if HR is active in this process. As an AML leader, you can influence the probability of internal fraud and conflicts of interest happening by encouraging the proper management of employees, as illustrated in Case Study 2.3 where diligence in a role was not rewarded, and 2.4 where a manager pays more attention to team social engagement than fulfilment of goals and objectives.

CASE STUDY 2.3: Where diligence is unrewarded

Murray was recruited five years ago as a technical specialist for the High Value Assets Company. At first, interested in his role, he was learning fast how to navigate the company systems and identify their connectivity. In the recruitment process, Murray was told that taking the role was a good career move as the manager of the section was looking to ensure succession planning, and his skills were just right to make him the candidate to be developed into the more senior role over the next couple of years.

Murray's first two years were coming to an end, and while he had been led to believe that HR had plans for his development, after his recruitment HR took no further interest in him, as that was the way it worked in the organization. He was a good performer in each appraisal cycle and that was where their interest finished. Murray was busy implementing new solutions for the company in his first years, and rather than chasing to ensure his attendance at the development training sessions planned for him by his manager, she did not encourage him but left him to work long hours to achieve a successful implementation that was well received in the business. In the meantime, his colleague Charles who was also on the shortlist for the promotion saw the opportunity, so he carried out the minimum of his own work possible to focus on the training sessions, putting his work burden on to his colleagues, which Murray would never do. The feedback that Charles gave to his manager on the sessions together with the links he made with his own work and hers convinced her that it was Charles and not Murray who was right for the promotion. It was too late when Murray saw this. He knew he was more skilful with greater expertise and diligence than Charles, but Charles walked off with the promotion 'prize'. Murray's disillusionment festered, and he increasingly determined to get his 'promotion' after all by manipulating those systems he was so diligent in mapping to give him a 'pay rise', and no one would know.

Questions

1. What visibility do you think your AML role has within your organization?
2. As manager or direct report, how much attention do you apply to just getting through the day to day?
3. Does your HR department engage in employee development?
4. As a manager, do you pay attention to the effectiveness of your team members in their current role when assessing them for future roles?
5. Do you consider that your treatment of team members will not give rise to resentments amongst them?

In Case Study 2.3, if Murray's HR partner had engaged in the development process, she may have recognized that to participate Murray needed some short-term assistance in implementing the new solution to give him time to attend training sessions, and level the playing field. Likewise, more attendance by the manager or HR could have ensured that Charles kept up with his work to enable a balanced view of achievements in the timescale. The likelihood is that Murray's sense of injustice against the organization will lead him to justify to himself taking what he likes in terms of time, resources or assets to make up for the disadvantage he feels he has suffered, which could have been avoided. Consider also the case of Enriquo in Case Study 2.4.

CASE STUDY 2.4: Reliance on technology v management oversight

Enriquo enjoyed his senior position as MLRO for Aspect Insurance. He was recruited into the position around two years ago. He had busy and varied activities to attend to each day and depended upon his direct reports to carry out their work with minimal supervision. Automated systems provided him with real-time reports on key metrics, and he felt that this was enough to ensure that the team was working well. Enriquo had his focus on building the team outside of working hours, and the group that regularly met tended to be those without dependants to care for at home and so were free to enjoy their socializing.

Enriquo was going through a particularly busy patch when Pedro, the new Investigation Manager, was recruited and on-boarded into his role, but his CV was good and Enriquo left him to settle in. After a while, Enriquo noticed that Pedro did not seem to always take note of his requests and guidance at work, but he was growing to be a popular member of the team's social events, and Enriquo was sure the work aspect would improve. Towards year end, Pedro still had not produced the final reports that Enriquo needed, but at his year-end appraisal, Enriquo classed him as a 'high performer' to avoid any cooling of his perceived friendship and team spirit, thinking he must address Pedro's performance in the coming months. They were busy months, and the trend continued, Pedro not delivering and Enriquo enjoying his camaraderie and turning a blind eye to failings in his work. As this continued, members of the team who worked well during working hours but were not members of the out of hours 'club' became increasingly disillusioned with Enriquo and their respect for him waned, along with their work ethic. By the time that Pedro's lack of performance was endangering Enriquo's ability to deliver on his own goals, division in the team was visible and HR was engaged in preparing a formal performance improvement plan for Pedro. Outraged at the suggestion his performance was inadequate, Pedro complained to HR: how could it be he was a poor performer when he was rated a high performer only a few months ago at appraisal? Nothing in his work had changed since then and he had the same manager, Enriquo, who had not mentioned any performance-related issues he could remember during his regular update meetings. Pedro knew that being on the performance improvement plan would mean he was no longer eligible to participate in the bonus scheme that year, which upset him very much. He suddenly found he was busy elsewhere out of working time, no longer socializing and commenting negatively to his work colleagues about those who did.

Questions

1. What on-boarding training do you have available for new hires? Is this left to HR or do you seek to track the establishment of new hires into your team?
2. Is your tendency as manager to pick up on performance issues and address them early on? If not, it may be helpful to partner with HR for, say, monthly one-to-ones to focus on team performance to prevent larger issues occurring.
3. Do you have one-to-ones with each of your team in which you provide constructive criticism and coaching where necessary? If team members know that you do this, you may find that they attend more closely to the deliverables of their role throughout the year.
4. Do you plan team social events based on what you would like to do yourself, or on the inclusion of as many of the team as possible? It may be that including informal lunchtime gatherings allow a greater number to attend.

In Case Study 2.4, the weak manager, Enriquo, was responsible for dismantling the structure of his AML compliance team and rendering it less effective in the process, by diverting the focus of his team interaction from engagement at work to personal allegiances. Variations of this scenario have played out several times in my experience, never with good outcomes, professionally, for management or for team members. When building and maintaining your AML team, their performance management is a priority to ensure that all aspects of AML compliance for which you are responsible are achieved. Reliance upon technology is not enough (see Chapter 6 for more).

Take time to ensure the role profiles of your AML team members are an accurate reflection of the role, that they have goals to achieve including clear deliverables, and manage them to that plan consistently. Management with no surprises is a mantra I follow: set out the plan, follow the plan, measure on the plan and provide rewards based on the achievement of the plan. Simple? That approach may lead to 'club' members being temporarily affronted by addressing their performance issues, but long term, in my view, it is worth remembering that consistency in performance management can help to build a cohesive team, which is more effective in managing the risk of the organization being used as a vehicle to launder the proceeds of crime.

Employee communications

The management and regularity of financial crime and AML employee communications will need to dovetail with other communications from various parts of the organization. It may be easier to achieve more regular communications by collaborating with these areas to provide a few words on the various aspects of AML controls rather than proliferating messages to employees that may remain unread in their e-mail inbox and become filtered into the 'Clutter' box instead. Cyber security messages fall into this category, for example:

> Protect the information on your computer and don't give your password to anyone. Remember that you will be held responsible for any activity that takes place on your computer. We in XYZ company carefully protect ourselves by verifying the identity of our customers to prevent our systems being abused to launder dirty money. Apply the same level of diligence to looking after the information and access that your computer provides and keep your password secure.

The development of an AML communications calendar can assist in mapping regular e-mail or intranet messages to employees throughout the year; see the example in Table 2.2. It may be that your organization already has an Internal Communications department. If so, in making your case for the inclusion of AML compliance messages you will have to find who 'owns' the process and from whom you will need approval to post the messages. Case Study 2.2, where Morgan

Table 2.2 AML communication plan

Quarter 1				
Topic	**Audience**	**Jan**	**Feb**	**March**
Step up to the AML year	All employees	✔		
Prior year statistics	Management	✔		
Enhancements to improve AML controls based on prior year*	All relevant employees		✔	
Hot topics: enhancements	All employees			✔

*Use the AML strategy wheel (Chapter 3) to risk assess, identify and implement enhancements, communicating them and providing training on their use at regular intervals.

Stanley was able to prove its diligence in providing anti-bribery and corruption messages that Garth Peterson ignored, demonstrates the worth of regular employee communications to the organization.

If your organization is of small to medium size, you may be able to carry out your communications plan by simply e-mailing relevant employees, and providing face-to-face AML updates at, say, quarterly intervals. However, in a larger organization with a Communications Team, you may have to negotiate your AML communications into their already sizeable plan. A well drafted plan that is signed off by the MLRO and senior manager in charge of Communications is harder to ignore than a plan drafted in the AML team and taken over to Communications to find open slots in their schedule.

Gaps and overlaps in prevention controls

The tendency to have gaps and overlaps in the AML and corruption prevention controls of an organization can be exacerbated or minimized by the structure of the organization itself. To illustrate this, consider the power structure of the following two corporations: Hyundai and John Lewis.

Hyundai

In a company with a hierarchical power structure at board level, such as Hyundai, the corporate structure is family-centric and paternalistic, with unfettered decision-making power being held by the dominant entrepreneur, in the South Korean *chaebol* structure. *Chaebol* is a Korean word made up of two words: *chae* (wealth) and *bol* (clan).

The chaebol system was introduced by collaboration between the South Korean government and family-owned local companies in the post-World War II era as a government-led initiative to stimulate economic regeneration. It produced huge chaebol companies such as Hyundai and Samsung, which operate with a hierarchical power structure at board level.

Although in the chaebol structure the board of directors may be informed, they may not be able to effectively exercise their responsibilities under the control of the dominant entrepreneur, and the importance of carrying out client due diligence and enhanced due diligence (see Chapter 4) in relevant arms of the organization may appear diminished in the face of the expectation of obedience to the guiding mind. This is quite the opposite of the recommendation of the UK Corporate Governance Code, which requires firms to separate out roles on the lines of ability, knowledge and skills, along the lines of stewardship theory, and so share the responsibility for strategic decision amongst a diverse group, bringing many informed views and experience, decreasing the risk of decision making.

John Lewis Partnership

By contrast to the example above is the UK-based John Lewis Partnership, an organization in which employees have an interest as shareholders in the firm and have their say in how it is run and managed. Since the 1920s, the beneficial owners of John Lewis have been the employees whose shares are held in trust. The corporate governance principles of fairness, democracy and transparency are embedded in the firm by this arrangement, as in all areas of the company employees are empowered by their shared ownership to have a strong voice, and the opportunities for risk minimization are enhanced throughout the company by its enlightened employee shareholders. They are aware of the risks in their area of responsibility as that is their work, and they actively engage in the mitigation of those risks on a day-to-day basis. This corporate structure is rare in profit-making organizations, and more often one can expect directors rather than shareholders to be the guiding minds in establishing effective controls. (More on the relevance of the corporate governance principles to minimizing the risk of your organization being used to launder the proceeds of crime can be found in Chapter 5.)

Collaboration between governance and business

Bringing the focus back to the organization of your obliged entity, as an AML leader you should ensure that you coordinate well with other governance functions to minimize the gaps and overlaps of AML compliance. Seek to recognize how the functions in the organization are managed by their leaders. Do they appear to work in isolation, becoming virtually impenetrable silos? These are the areas that are least likely to be open to change and collaboration when new requirements are made of them when regulations change. The pull of the familiar to remain the same is, in my experience, immense. This is where your work at writing policies to the benefit of the business areas as well as remaining true to regulatory requirements helps your AML de-risking focus to become a reality. It may take time, sometimes years, to achieve the compliance goal, but your patience and persistent attention will help you to achieve 'baby steps' along the way. We all know that the first steps are the most tentative, but they become more confident and stronger in time, especially when the 'baby' is fed a healthy diet and has the opportunity to grow with the programme!

Researching your policies and procedures also gives you the opportunity to view them objectively in comparison to those of other departments. Challenges that arise if their areas of responsibility overlap with yours should be welcomed as a way to review their relevance, and for developing your network of colleagues across functions. In my view any recognition of gaps or overlaps in policy or procedure is an opportunity for improvement and collaboration, growing the spirit of walking together even if there are setbacks along the way.

Key takeaways

- There is an inherent link between the strategy of an organization and its risk appetite that will act to guide the sort of risks that senior management will expect to deal with; these differ across industries.
- When you mobilize to manage risks, including AML, look for how your governance controls may impact strategy. Always remaining on the right side of legal and regulatory compliance, design your controls with the business and implement them to maximize their benefit to the business.

- Well written and categorized role profiles are the keystone of good employee management. By starting with clear expectations, employees can work to their goal achievement from day one. Managers can use the role profiles to better assess the balance and adequacy of their team with reference to the expectations set on them by the organization.
- Time spent on managing an effective AML training plan will not only hone the training of the AML professionals involved, it will also clearly inform employees of the expectations the organization has of them in combating money laundering and act as a defence in the event that employee fraud or corruption including money laundering is taking place.
- There are many methods of performance management and certainly one size does not fit all. However, as an AML manager, I have found that performance management for team building, collaboration and attention to detail that gives employees the confidence to raise issues and suggest improvements is a very productive way of maximizing the effectiveness of the AML team.
- Ensuring your employee communications programme is effective pays dividends in safeguarding the organization from rogue employee activity. It also encourages the Communications team to regard AML compliance messages as mainstream, to be regularly scheduled, rather than ad hoc and fitted in for distribution when a gap in their schedule allows.
- Gaps and overlaps in the management structure of an organization are as important to identify as those between departments and individuals. There is always a tendency to have gaps and overlaps, so your constant awareness will help you to minimize the risk of your organization being used by the corrupt for laundering money.

References and further reading

Financial Reporting Council (2016) The UK Corporate Governance Code, available at: www.frc.org.uk/directors/corporate-governance-and-stewardship/uk-corporate-governance-code (last accessed 30 January 2018)

Fox, T (2012) Morgan Stanley Gets Thumbs up from DOJ & SEC For Best Practices Compliance Program, *Dallas: Corporate Compliance Insights*, May

John Lewis Partnership (2017) *The Constitution of the John Lewis Partnership*, John Lewis Partnership, London

The Foreign Corrupt Practices Act of 1977, as amended, 15 U.S.C. §§78dd-1, et seq. (FCPA)

Tricker, B (2009) *Corporate Governance: Principles, policies and practices*, Oxford University Press, Oxford

United States Sentencing Commission, Guidelines Manual, §3E1.1 (November 2016) www.int-comp.org/qualifications/all-certificates-and-diplomas/www.int-comp.org/qualifications/all-certificates-and-diplomas/ (last accessed 25 March 2017)

US v Garth Peterson, No. 12-cr-224 (E.D.N.Y. 2012) www.int-comp.org/qualifications/all-certificates-and-diplomas/ (last accessed 25 March 2017)

Using the anti-money laundering strategy wheel

03

This chapter covers:

- Governance guidance to organizations.
- The anti-money laundering strategy wheel.
- Policy and training.
- Awareness and commitment.
- Prevention and detection.
- Whistleblowing and investigation.
- Monitoring and review.
- Inherent roadblocks.
- Carrots and sticks.
- Encouraging engagement

Governance guidance to organizations

As discussed in Chapter 1, the money laundering bodies and regulations were originally put in place to prevent the proceeds of drug crime flowing through primarily financial services businesses, and the reach of anti-money laundering (AML) regulation has now spread to an extended list of sectors and industries. The principles and practices set out in AML regulation are a useful guide to profit- and non-profit-making organizations all over the world, setting out clear guidelines on forming protective governance. Even if you are outside the regulated sector and did not know that your business was being used to launder the proceeds of crime, you may still be held accountable for letting it happen and be subject to law enforcement activity. Increased international attention to businesses outside of financial services has already stretched to gaming, accountancy, real estate and company services businesses. It is quite possible that your organization may become an obliged entity in time, and may be held accountable in the event that an employee uses the business systems and infrastructure to perpetrate fraud or money laundering. Also, if laundered money is found in an organization it can be reclaimed by a country's competent authorities with no compensation paid to the organization, whether or not it is in the regulated sector. In large corporations such as Siemens in Case Study 3.1 this may not present an issue and some may have made provision to deal with such inconvenient matters, but for small to medium businesses it can make the difference between profitability and receivership.

CASE STUDY 3.1: Siemens

Siemens, having been found by the US Securities and Exchange Commission, US Department of Justice and European authorities to be participating in bribery and corruption in multiple locations across the world, won for itself a fine of $1.6 billion in 2008. This was after admitting its guilt in taking part in corruption in close to 20 countries as far apart as Argentina and Poland, Malaysia and Germany. Comprehensive institutional corruption was exposed. The range of industries across which its corrupt activities spread was impressive too: alleged impropriety in a telecom contract for the Olympic Games in Greece in 2004, anti-trust violations in the Israeli electricity market, bribes paid for a multi-million hospital equipment contract in Vietnam... the list is long!

Now, $1.6 billion makes a dent in the profitability of even a huge multinational such as Siemens, and CEO Peter Loscher brought in a new senior management team including Peter Solmssen as General Counsel to assist in cleaning up the organization's institutional culture. Peter Solmssen's premise is that to have sustainability it is not only necessary to have clean air and clean water, but a clean economic system too, one that works for everyone. He argues that sustainability means having responsible citizens, both corporate and individual. That is such a big move from operating with the systemic corruption that permeated Siemens, and it called for a fundamental change in the culture of the firm. How to stop employees habitually engaging in bribery and corruption? How could Peter Loscher clearly indicate that those engaged in bribery were to stop immediately?

What he did was to promise that anyone who came forward to admit their involvement in bribery would get a full amnesty, even to the point of providing company-backed assistance to any employee whose admission led to legal problems. In terms of culture, many a fundamentally honest person can become persuaded to engage in corruption when his or her livelihood depends upon it, becoming a guilty party. Thinking in terms of taking responsibility (Peter Loscher was CEO at the time the corruption was taking place), this step, together with replacing 80 per cent of top tier management and 70 per cent of middle management, essentially embraced Siemens' executive management responsibility and commitment to change. The deal was that if, however, anyone who was involved in the bribery did not come forward and their activity was discovered later, they would be fired. A staggering 130 employees were reported as coming forward to admit their role in bribery!

The question now is: what impact did ceasing to operate with a business model of bribery have on Siemens' bottom line? General Counsel, Peter Solmssen's message to the United Nations (UN) Global Compact Leaders' Summit in September 2017 was clear: an important outcome from the Siemens case is that in ceasing to engage in bribery and corruption to win deals, *their bottom line has not suffered.* Quite the reverse: Siemens reported year-on-year revenue growth between 2010 and 2012, giving the strong message to other organizations that clean business is good business.

Bribery and corruption are, of course, global problems and they need a global solution. What the Siemens case has shown is that if global organizations in a market agree not to give bribes or give in to corruption during their business activity, they can be instrumental in reducing the impact of corruption while retaining profitability.

Questions

1. Do you believe that the AML controls in your organization are robust enough to prevent it from paying bribes to acquire new business?
2. What is the attitude of your senior management when you ask them to change working practices to comply with AML regulation?
3. What will you respond if they answer, 'So what will happen if we don't comply?'
4. Do you believe that the tone of your senior management is one of adherence to relevant laws and regulation, or the desire to circumvent them where possible?

There is more on cultural change in Chapter 8, which will expand on the tools that AML professionals can use to drive cultural change. Let us benefit from the lessons of the Siemens example, which illustrates that as well as bribery and corruption not actually benefiting an organization financially, a tone of adherence to AML compliance requirements from the top really counts. It is also important to have a plan, and that is where the AML strategy wheel comes in.

AML strategy wheel

Although it may seem like a cost of resource to the business to identify and draft an AML strategy, if it includes training, practical steps, monitoring and regular reviews its very existence will alert potential criminal elements in your organization that you are not ignorant of the risks. It will also make their colleagues aware. This has the effect of raising the risk factor for those likely to take advantage of AML loopholes and management blind spots that could be used for criminal purposes, and reducing the tendency to exploit them.

Your AML strategy foundations will be built on a risk-based approach as required by regulation. Risk assessments themselves can vary in their complexity according to the activities of the organization and, as discussed in Chapters 5 and 6, these will include:

- country risk;
- people risk;
- product risk; and
- delivery channel risk.

The AML strategy wheel in Figure 3.1 is a device that I have found helpful in thinking about the primary activities the AML leader may wish to include on a regular basis, to grow AML risk awareness and compliance. Its elements are those of governance and risk management, with focused steps to reduce the risk of fraud and money laundering occurring within the organization, and from external threats using the systems of your organization for money laundering

Figure 3.1 The AML strategy wheel

purposes. Using the AML strategy wheel, you will be able to better articulate your control framework. Clear articulation brings more willing supporters and, as discussed below, inclusion brings engagement, both of which are essentials in establishing your AML control environment.

You may prefer visualizing your AML strategy with more areas than those in Figure 3.1, splitting out, say, policy from training, to provide a step-by-step approach to the improvement strategy cycle. Revise and renew your policy, training and prevention measures in the light of review and monitoring. Assess the risk based on findings and new threats to the business.

Stop and think

Thinking about reducing the risk of your organization being used as a vehicle to launder the proceeds of crime, how would you implement your AML strategy? Include the at-risk departments, relevant stakeholders and management tools you have at your disposal.

Policy and training

Once the company strategy and goals are set at board level and communicated to the business, it is the turn of policies and their associated procedures to take centre stage. It is worth taking the time to discover how other governance functions such as Internal Audit, Finance and Cyber Security are managing the risks they perceive from their own points of view, as collaboration with them could strengthen AML controls using existing infrastructure.

When creating your AML policies, think of them as the enactment of primary legislation of your AML control environment. Especially in a multinational organization, they will need to embrace international best practice to apply as a global standard, which you may be asked to disclose to contracting third parties in due course. They need to be written broadly enough to withstand minor regulatory changes without amendment, have a policy review cycle with a period long enough to satisfy resourcing of amendment review, and short enough to satisfy auditors that the policy is up to date. Clarity of language will help employees to appreciate the policies' relevance to their role. Your AML policy should fit in to the 'family' of other policies in your organization to provide a clear and articulate governance suite by which to operate. Identify and speak to your audience when writing policies; this is equally applicable when designing procedures.

Stop and think

How much time is spent by AML compliance in preparing your employee training? Does it provide the training you need to protect your organization and your AML Responsible Officer (RO)?

Procedures that make up the framework of the AML control environment are your 'secondary legislation', filling in the specifics of required activities and easier to amend when changes occur. You will clearly need to keep your finger on the pulse of AML regulatory change affecting your industry and scan your risk horizon for external changes that may affect your organization. Equally, you will need to maintain internal relationships with the business areas in which your AML controls operate to ensure that risk of their failure by becoming obsolete due to changing business models or data software changes is minimized.

Your AML policy and procedures form the basis of controls that make up your first line of defence in preventing criminals from using your organization as a vehicle to launder the proceeds of their crimes. Training, as discussed in Chapter 2, provides the best practice guidance for organizations to follow. In my view, training courses are never the 'final' training course, but the iteration issued at the time to always be improved upon and updated at the next delivery. As AML threats and examples emerge over time, they can in my experience be more easily incorporated into the training programme and more readily provide updated guidance.

Awareness and commitment

Developing an articulate AML control environment is one thing; communicating it in an effective way is an art peculiar to those used to giving employees work that they are not necessarily willing to do, with authority. It is all about influencing the culture of the organization. In my experience, in changing the culture of a business nothing is more positively powerful for an AML RO than having the active and visible commitment of the CEO and senior management to a clearly articulated, meaningful strategy to protect a company's reputation and therefore its value. (Effecting cultural change is discussed more fully in Chapter 8.)

Each communication should speak to the audience for which it is intended. If you recognize that you have several audiences, which is more than likely, you may wish to tailor your communications for them, and split them out as in the example below:

Introduction of AML controls

To whom? All employees.

By whom? CEO (Celebrity winner!)

How? E-mail to all employees setting out commitment of organization to comply with legislation. Clear expectations (compliance of all employees), authoritative, directional.

Introducing controls for departments

To whom? Relevant employees.

By whom? Department manager.

How? Clear and authoritative, introducing procedural controls.

Detailed controls and allocation of responsibilities

To whom? Team members.

By whom? Team leaders.

How? Having been given authority by senior and line management, team leaders can empower team members to act with authority, as designated.

Management information

To whom? Senior leadership.

By whom? Responsible Officer.

How? Data derived from controls, providing objective records of compliance achieved and improvements required.

All that work! And where does it get you on the celebrity scale? Fourth!

Prevention and detection

Prevention of AML risks crystallizing is for ever at the forefront of the diligent AML professional's mind, no matter what role they occupy. The eternal prevention questions trouble sleep and occupy countless working hours:

- Who needs to be involved in establishment of policy and procedure, review and monitoring, remediation...?
- How to structure the training plan, CDD arrangements, monitoring programme, data reporting, etc.
- What are the elements to include in business plans, CDD data analysis, AML software selection...?
- Where are the funds and employee resources coming from to establish the controls and provide regular monitoring and remediation?

- Why do we newly need the AML controls and monitoring? Clear justification of expenses incurred may well help to smooth the path?
- When do we need to implement AML controls, carry out review and monitoring?
- How can AML compliance dovetail in to the rhythm of activities in other governance functions?

The whole AML prevention strategy is in place to minimize the risk of your organization being used to launder the proceeds of crime, so it needs to be robust. However, when control systems fail, as they inevitably do, a plan for dealing with issues when they are detected must be there in advance. What might that plan look like? For a basic AML issues log, see Table 3.1.

Table 3.1 would be a subset of your more detailed action plan, used for reporting purposes to retain confidentiality of the issues raised, while including planned completion dates as well as those achieved. A far more detailed log could be owned by your AML team to ensure that each item to be addressed is completed. The aim here is that when you have detected an issue, each of the elements that make it up are noted and remediation activity forms the action plan to prevent further issues of that kind occurring, as far as possible. Data gathered from your AML log on the where, when, what, why, how and who of the issue can provide the basis for management information for your monitoring team onto the areas of highest detected risk. Issues detected may alert you to failing procedures, or absence of agreed policy and procedure to deal with activities your organization carries out.

Table 3.1 AML issues log

Issue Reference	Date received	Allocated to	Remediation activity	Planned completion date	Completion date achieved	Audit report delivered
12978	dd/mm/yyyy	Named resource	Select category of activity	dd/mm/yyyy	dd/mm/yyyy	dd/mm/yyyy

Taking the approach of dealing with root causes of AML issues and not just the symptoms as they happen may mean keeping the item open for longer. However, keeping an item open while its underlying cause is dealt with will mean the item is less likely to recur, leaving your team capacity to focus their attention on new threats or failures in the future. So the AML strategy wheel can better be described as in Figure 3.2, as several smaller improvement cycles driving forward AML governance, especially during the stages of detection and prevention, whistleblowing and investigation, and monitoring and review.

AML activity can demonstrably make a difference in reducing the organizational risk of being used as a vehicle for money laundering, which is then expressed in policies, training and communications. The environment this creates – an upward spiral of improvement – is far more exciting for AML professionals to contribute to than one where superficial issues are fixed quickly leaving the underlying cause intact to visit another day. Not many employees thrive on hamster wheels!

Figure 3.2 AML strategy, wheels within wheels

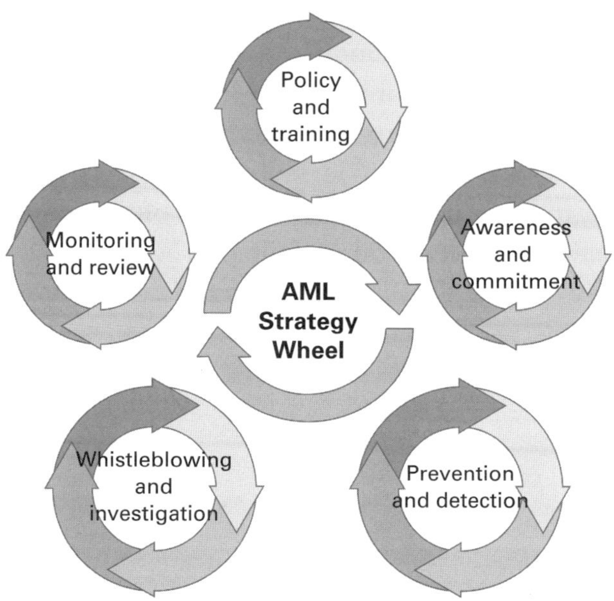

Whistleblowing and investigation

Occasionally, potential AML breaches and issues are raised via the whistleblowing hotline. If your organization does not have one as yet, however small it is, I believe a hotline is worth implementing. Giving all employees a way to confidentially air a view or express a concern on something that is going on in the organization can open the eyes of busy people who are not looking that way, but are otherwise interested. Having a statement in your Code of Conduct that every employee is responsible for reporting matters that breach the organization's Code that he or she becomes aware of may help to encourage reporting. However, in some cultures reporting others' activity is seen in a very dim light, which will inevitably take time to overcome. In my experience, employees fraudulently using company credit cards, misusing the expenses system and criminal customers bragging about their activity have all been reported via the confidential whistleblowing line. In each case the confidentiality of the reporter has been protected as a priority, and all underlying issues addressed to prevent a recurrence of the issue.

Reporter protection throughout an investigation helps to ensure that there is minimal possibility for retaliation, and where this is applied consistently, employee confidence in reporting tends to grow. Being able to report confidentially helps employees report suspect activities that they think are 'odd' or 'surely against the Code of Conduct' in a safe environment. In Chapter 5 you will read the case study of Janice, Personal Assistant to Peter, a senior manager who signs off on a deal without having due diligence completed. With an effective whistleblowing hotline, Janice may not have just shrugged and thought her boss must be right. The very existence of a whistleblowing hotline may have caused manager Peter to pause and wonder what he would do if his avoidance of carrying out the due diligence were reported, saving himself and the company the pain of a failed deal, avoidable simply by carrying out the organization's standard client due diligence (CDD).

Monitoring and review

The monitoring and review we discuss here relate to the procedures backed by the policies that define them, rather than the CDD discussed in Chapter 4. The content of AML compliance monitoring depends on the nature of controls placed on areas of the organization to satisfy regulation. There is a high degree of information and data management involved, which in itself has come under increased scrutiny in the light of cyber threats and enactment of the European Union's General Data Protection Regulation. In small organizations, it may be that manual processes are most appropriate, bearing in mind cost-effectiveness, but in medium-sized organizations up to the largest multinational enterprises, it is likely that computer software is deployed to effectively monitor and manage data.

In all my AML compliance monitoring experience, I have never found that the results of a first monitoring exercise show that adequate procedures are in place. They are usually woefully deficient, and because of this it appears that early monitoring of AML procedures is *de rigeur!* In the first stages of testing a new AML compliance control environment, the results may show that months of work are needed to embed the control, but they are the starting point from which all improvement must flow. Because of this, presenting them positively to senior management, perhaps with the percentage of success towards adequate procedures, will help to focus their attention. Adding next steps as the larger part of the AML status report will probably serve you better than dwelling on the points of failure. It is too soon. The business areas will learn. So will you, and from this AML controls become more finely tuned with greater take-up in the business. If they do not, and every effort has been made to train and communicate the AML controls in the business, then it will be time to implement sanctions.

Stop and think

Do reports of financial crime and money laundering raised by your whistleblowing hotline form part of AML information-gathering activity?

Inherent roadblocks

Where a company has been in existence for a number of years, growing rapidly with all attention focused on profitability and moving forwards, there is likely to be a whole body of employees who have worked in the business for several years carrying out their work in their own way. These groups are especially hard to bring along with new requirements of regulation as the scope of AML creeps ever wider. They may resist all attempts to train for competence, and not wish to comply with new processes even when they are clearly defined, trained out and monitored. These are likely to be the very people who think themselves exempt from change, leaving risk exposure to money laundering, and this group is highly likely to find reasons not to comply, as discussed in Chapter 4. This tendency is even greater in a multinational seeking to implement AML controls in branches or subsidiaries when the local country culture is one where corruption is evident by government officials and is pervasive in local society. Consider the roadblocks set before Joseph in Case Study 3.2, when he joined Robson Company Services just before its initial public offering (IPO).

CASE STUDY 3.2: Linkage between policy drafting and effectiveness

A multinational enterprise, Robson Company Services, employed Joseph as its new RO for AML in preparation for improving its governance in advance of an IPO. Joseph's first task was to evaluate what policies were available in the business. Finding that the policies were not actually written for Robson Company Services, but appeared to be written on a template by lawyers whose first interest was not plain English, and who clearly did not understand the nature of the firm, Joseph set about a radical revision. He engaged with in-house lawyers and business line owners to re-draft and re-focus the policies to be relevant and clear in their meaning. Risk assessing from a fraud and money laundering point of view, Joseph started with the Anti-bribery and Financial Crime Policy.

> **Note**
>
> Policies must be clearly written and practical so that employees actually know what they mean and use them as a point of reference in the quest to reduce operational risk.

The same approach had been applied to Code of Conduct annual training, where a company providing scenarios of right and wrong behaviour was retained. None of the Robson Company Services policies were referenced in the training and neither was there a call to action for the employees.

> **Note**
>
> Each company is different, and although clearly they will be complying with their local country laws and, if they are a multinational, hopefully with international soft law, if the training does not appear to be relevant to employees they will rush through it as quickly as possible and the opportunity to engage the workforce to assist in minimizing fraud and AML risk will be wasted. Take the time to research and write the training your organization needs.

What was included, however, was a form the employees had to sign to confirm they would follow all of the policies of the company: the ones that were bordering on indecipherable to the majority of people and which, therefore, had no practical purpose.

> **Note**
>
> Although certification to policies is commendable and alerts employees to the importance of the policies in their work, in the event of disciplinary action being taken against them for a policy breach, the employee may rightly claim that the policy was irrelevant as it did not provide them with clear guidance on how to address the particular operational risk.

Joseph soon discovered that he was also responsible for investigating breaches of the Code of Conduct, and within a month of joining the firm he was flying from his London head office to Buenos Aires to investigate the misuse of company assets by the senior sales manager, Louis. In preparation for the visit Joseph looked for the Spanish version of the Code of Conduct, but Robson Company Services had minimized its costs of production and maintenance by not having it translated from English at all, despite having a decentralized operational model. In Buenos Aires, Louis claimed not to know that he could not use the company's premises and facilities to set up and run his cash-based family business. Pretending at first not to understand English, his immediate boss also appeared on the scene, which improved his understanding no end. Initially Louis did not know whether to be delighted or dismayed at his dilemma, as AML Compliance was paying him a visit and no one from head office had ever done so before.

Note

It is highly likely that employees of branches or subsidiaries in higher-risk countries (as identified by Transparency International) are more influenced by the culture of their country than by documents written in a foreign language by the company they work for. For governance to be effective, the people whose behaviour one seeks to guide have to be engaged. That means taking an interest in them, communicating at least in part in their language and helping them to understand what is required. Encouraging their thinking to embrace the controls introduced to reduce risks within the company is a key element, and that includes the risk of the company being used by criminals as a vehicle via which to launder money. As a general rule of thumb, even where the lingua franca of a multinational is English, where contracts of employment and everyday business is carried out in the local language, that is the language that is understood and that matters.

Only a few months later, a situation revealed itself in Vienna where another country manager was fraudulently using company systems to benefit his own family business, and had interlinked payments for social and business activity to such an extent that even Mother's Day flowers were being paid for by the firm.

Joseph was ever more aware that the combination of a lack of engagement with a decentralized business model was increasing the potential for fraud and money laundering. Robson Company Services was relying not on carrots, but on the stick of disciplinary action should wrongdoing be discovered. All very well, but if the errant local manager is well known in his industry, the potential for him to move to a competitor and take with him insider knowledge of the firm is high. Better to engage with local managers and modify their behaviour before the bad practices set in, rather than clean up the mess afterwards.

Questions

1. Are all of the AML-related policies in your organization written in a clear and understandable manner, with relevant guidance?
2. If your organization is multinational, are your AML policies available in the local language wherever possible, or are they just in English?
3. Does your organization have employees with the knowledge and skills to write tailored AML policies and training, or is this outsourced?
4. If outsourced, how can you ensure that your AML training and policies look relevant to your organization?

The inherent roadblocks described in Case Study 3.2 are typical of those encountered by AML professionals, and even though they show that implementing controls for AML compliance can be anything but simple, identifying them provides direction. Below is a list of example roadblocks and suggested opportunities for better collaboration and effectiveness in establishing AML controls:

Poorly written policies

Short term: Engage with in-house lawyers and business leaders to match the policies to the activities of the organization, clearly and concisely.

Medium term: Establish a policy control document, capturing which stakeholder 'owns' which sections of the relevant policy. Agree with senior management the term of a policy review cycle.

Long term: Using your policy control document for reference, engage with identified stakeholders to review the policies on a regular basis, within the review cycle.

Undocumented procedures creating single point failures

Short term: Identify as far as possible the procedures relevant to AML and their owners. Engage with line management of the owner, to agree where a refresh would be beneficial to AML controls.

Medium term: Engage with procedure owners and their manager to introduce enhanced procedures, covering AML control requirements.

Long term: Provide AML compliance support to procedure owners, liaise to produce effective management information and further enhancements as required.

Resistance to adoption of new processes by long-term employees

Short term: Once identified, make as early a start as possible, engaging with line management to promote the change.

Medium term: If resistance continues, escalate. It may be that the resistant party is the only person who really knows the process, and line management may struggle to influence. Record attempts made to influence, and pushback received.

Long term: Continued resistance now will be having an impact on AML compliance. Use the management information gathered in the medium term to engage HR and senior management in resolving the resistance.

Lack of investment in relevant software

Short term: Liaise with procurement and business areas to research providers.

Medium term: Trial software and install. Test and introduce software to relevant functions.

Long term: Review effectiveness of software.

Unwillingness to mandate training completions

Short term: Launch training with sponsorship by senior management. Track AML training completions within the training period.

Medium term: Provide support to late completers, including their manager. Create management information on AML training completions. Relate this to hours spent in follow up to 100 per cent completions.

Long term: Present management information gathered in the medium term to senior management. With their sponsorship, introduce sanctions on employees who do not complete, for example, limiting the grade they can achieve at appraisal, docking a percentage of bonus.

Stop and think

Think about the inherent roadblocks that there may be in your organization. Make a list of what they are and describe the actions you can take to manage or overcome them. Not all of your actions have to be 'quick fixes,' so put them into what you think are achievable timescales:

Short term: between one and six months.

Medium term: between six months and two years.

Long term: between two and five years.

Consider the example roadblocks above and the suggested opportunities for better collaboration with colleagues to improve the effectiveness of you and your team when establishing AML controls in your organization.

Carrots and sticks

Improvements, including remedial activity, can all fall into the two categories of carrots and sticks when applied to AML compliance. We know as AML professionals that we need to get the business to buy in to AML governance controls, to leave the organization with as little risk as possible of being used as a vehicle to launder the proceeds of crime, and to ensure we are keeping on the compliant side of regulatory requirements to avoid being caught up in mandatory reviews and remediation from competent authorities. Carrots, or encouragement, guidance and practical help towards achieving compliant status do tend to have an appetizing quality that brings individuals and departments onside with AML Compliance.

Note

Carrots are more appetizing than sticks.

However, when the only recourse is to apply a stick, mandating activity or implementing a longer process, maintaining positivity and a professional demeanour is the way forward. There is no need for apology when AML Compliance needs to act in order to minimize the risk of the organization being used to launder the proceeds of crime. Quite the reverse. As AML professionals we are not sorry to implement business-focused solutions to keep the organization safe; we are only sorry that the business is not as enthusiastic as we are about minimizing AML risk.

> **Note**
>
> Sticks may become essential when carrots fail to provide results.

Try to foresee the roadblocks that may be placed in your path by those who object, and visualize whether they are protecting their long undisturbed empire with vigour, or maybe they have really found a flaw in your plans. Whoever it is objecting, work to ensure a successful outcome, with greater respect for each other. In this way, over time, you will be influencing others on the basis of professional trust, and they will gradually see the benefits in the more AML-compliant aspect of the organization.

Carrots

Taking the view that most employees are good citizens, willing to comply with the policies of your organization and doing their best to ensure its success, clear guidance as to what good looks like, or carrots, is an essential element of AML compliance strategy. Carrots help to win over hearts and minds, creating engagement and improved diligence in employees. Identifying just what those carrots might be is a matter of time and research from the RO and his or her team. Data gained from carrying out investigations into policy breaches can provide useful information on where weaknesses in the AML programme may exist. No one knows the weaknesses better than the employees and third parties who use them every day, and if they think that the RO neither knows nor cares about them, they are likely to be exploited. Good people can turn into fraudsters and money launderers just by virtue of the fact that opportunity is before them and temptation draws them on, unnoticed, as in Case Study

1.1 where aeroplane maintenance workers were stealing lost property just because they could. This realization provides a very good reason for the AML compliance team to find these weaknesses and improve the governance around them to reduce the risk of tempting otherwise good employees into wrongdoing. Applying positive energy provides momentum, and whereas AML compliance activity may be seen as a cost without adding value, the time spent in honing governance activity to provide fixes for weaknesses helps to drive the AML de-risking mission forwards and bring the commitment of the organization with you.

Taking the time to write and produce tailored training for the organization online, and for face-to-face delivery to high-risk groupings, pays dividends. Those who take the training are not only aware of the potential for systems or products being used for wrongdoing, but are actively making it the responsibility of those using the systems or products to themselves be the gatekeepers.

In a multinational organization, providing local language communications of key information, including AML and anti-bribery and corruption requirements, is another way to impress upon employees wherever they are and whatever the local cultural norms that the governance controls apply to them too. This can be introduced as a positive contribution to offices in regions remote from the organizational hub. Employees in these offices may feel cut off and forgotten, and where head office has taken the time to produce local language communications, it will not be lost on the local language reader that it is important for them to understand what they are being told. If this is not possible, head office AML compliance networking with individuals who hold key regional or country responsibilities gives encouragement for outliers to engage with governance activity and have their efforts noticed.

Carrots come in all shapes and sizes. Consider the encouragements in Figure 3.3 when designing your own. Cultivate your carrots! A healthy crop, distributed with generous discretion, will raise AML compliance awareness in a positive way, maximizing employee buy-in.

Figure 3.3 Carrots

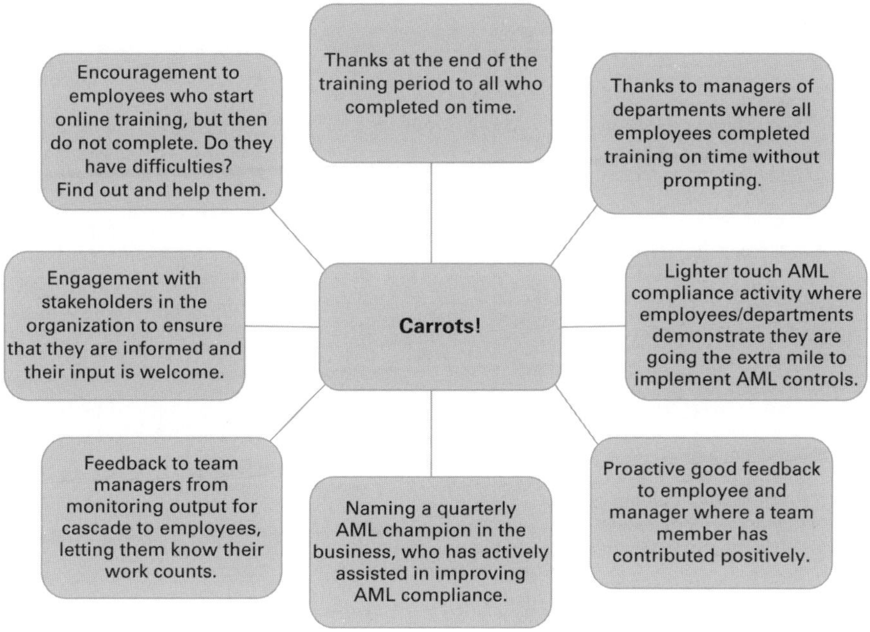

Sticks

In my experience in AML compliance, sticks work well in the short term, but in the longer term they can result in harboured resentment in employees and, apart from in cases of egregious non-compliance, the use of sticks is unlikely to win over the hearts and minds of people in your organization to better engage with AML controls. Being averse to implementing the sticks of disciplinary action, withdrawal of bonus payments and the like is, in my view, a good place to start, but having them in your armoury is essential. Figure 3.4 contains suggestions of potentially effective sticks. Implementing these will require liaison with HR and line management, so your efforts in establishing good relationships when producing business-focused policies and procedures will pay dividends when you have to engage in remedial activities.

Figure 3.4 Sticks

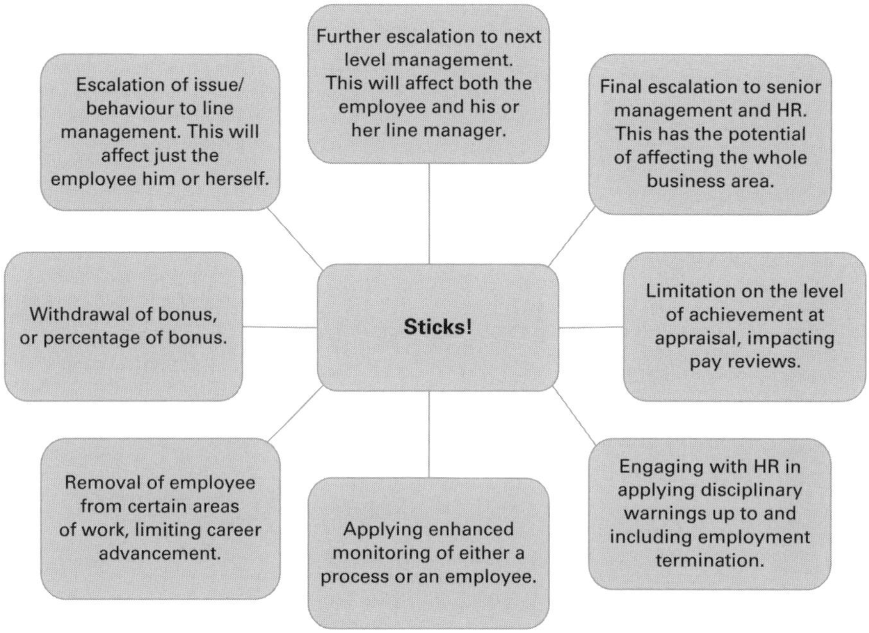

Aim to use all the appropriate carrots you have before deploying sticks. Adhering to a new AML compliance control environment is unlikely to be high on anyone's preferred activity list in the business, so in creating a positive implementation regime you have a greater chance of being noted for your diplomacy!

Stop and think

What are the carrots and sticks for employee behaviour in your organization? Are they effective? How might they change?

Encouraging engagement

The AML strategy wheel articulates an AML team's activities in such a way as to encourage engagement of all members of the team. No matter if they are 'just' writing policies or training, or 'only' working on investigations, if the work of team members is recognized as a valuable part of the output of the team, the senior AML professional is likely to achieve more progress in reducing organizational risk by the efforts of the motivated team.

However, the perceived sponsorship of AML controls in your organization is also a matter of strategy. In our view there is no place for an RO wanting to satisfy a wish for glory when introducing an AML strategy into a newly obliged organization. If it appears that the AML RO is the sponsor, it is more likely to appear that compliance requirements come from that department alone, without sponsorship from the top. Having the CEO or Chief Risk Officer herald their support of the initiative will provide clear indication of their sponsorship of AML controls to all employees. Fully informed of the legislation and its effect on the organization, they will demonstrate senior management buy-in as sponsor of AML compliance activity and indicate commitment of the whole organization. When periodic awareness notifications and training are launched, it is clear that all departments are subject to the controls the training describes, and employees are less likely to feel that they are outside of the AML control framework and 'invisible'.

Key takeaways

- In providing governance guidance to organizations, the 'tone from the top' counts. Using your version of the AML strategy wheel will provide you with an AML control environment you can articulate well.
- In your attempts at communicating awareness of and gaining commitment to your AML control environment, using the tone from the top spreads the word faster.
- Clarity of purpose and language in your policies and training provides a dependable basis for your AML controls. Keeping policies consistent with reality better demonstrates the organization's commitment to implementing a practical AML control environment.
- Prevention and detection work hand-in-hand at the front line of AML compliance. Your controls are there to prevent the organization being

used as a money laundering vehicle, and your detection work helps to pick up where criminals create a space in between the controls, requiring you to implement further prevention measures.

- Although whistleblowing and investigation are not generally regarded as core activities of AML controls, they can be very useful in raising awareness of issues. Log relevant actions to address the issues raised and use them to improve the AML control environment.
- Providing senior management with the information they need from AML monitoring pays the dividend of documenting activities of your AML control environment. It articulates the need for review of controls upon which senior management can make decisions and more readily sponsor AML activities.
- Inherent roadblocks will almost inevitably emerge once changes to AML procedures are announced. Dealing with them in a measured and progressive way will give you a better chance of effecting cultural change, especially where long-standing employees have disproportionate influence.
- Carrots work better than sticks when introducing AML control activities, at least at first, as they produce more willing adherence to new controls as well as better employee engagement with the AML compliance team. Should the use of sticks be necessary, using them sparingly in collaboration with other governance functions, notably HR, will provide consistency of disciplinary activity across the organization and demonstrate that AML compliance is mainstream and not an optional extra.

References and further reading

Campbell, N J (1998) *Writing Effective Policies and Procedures: A step-by-step resource for clear communication*, AMACOM, New York

Montgomery, C A (2012) *The Strategist: Be the leader your business needs*, Harper Collins, New York

Schafer, D (2008) Siemens to pay €1bn fines to close bribery scandal, 15/12, *Financial Times*, available from: www.ft.com/content/1cc029de-cae9-11dd-87d7-000077b07658 (last accessed 25 January 2018)

SEC v Siemens Aktiengesellschaft (2008) 1:08-cv-02167

Watson, B (2013) Siemens and the battle against bribery and corruption, 18/9, *The Guardian*, available from: http://www.corruptie.org/siemens-and-the-battle-against-bribery-and-corruption-2/ (last accessed 25 January 2018)

Applying the brakes at key moments

04

In this chapter, while looking into the steps obliged entities must take to ensure they know who they are doing business with and where funds passing through them are coming from, think of the anti-money laundering strategy wheel in Chapter 3 and how the different elements link together.

This chapter covers:

- Client due diligence (CDD).
- Enhanced due diligence (EDD).
- Correspondent banking and reliance on third parties.
- Politically exposed persons (PEPs).
- Simplified due diligence (SDD).
- Summary of notable changes in the Fourth European Union Anti-Money Laundering Directive (4MLD).

The increasing legislative developments discussed in Chapter 1 led to the need for obliged entities to devise and implement risk-based AML controls in their organizations. Building blocks of the governance environment that encourages them to grow and strategies that can help to embed them are discussed in Chapters 2 and 3, and this chapter is all about the controls themselves: how to apply the brakes at key moments of the customer journey.

Both profit-making and fundraising organizations benefit from ensuring that their systems and controls provide a robust braking system to prevent their employees from rushing into arrangements without checking with whom they are doing business. Of course, all obliged entities have to implement controls to prevent laundered money passing through their systems. Regulated industries have their own specific elements to consider when introducing AML controls, and taking a risk-based approach, as discussed in Chapter 5, allows obliged entities the flexibility to make appropriate decisions to manage the risks of their own business. When new regulations such as 4MLD come into effect, they provide the cutting edge of AML measures to better manage present-day risks as identified by the Financial Action Task Force (FATF). These new measures serve to highlight refinements to the AML braking system. They are summarized at the end of this chapter to provide a checklist to add to your systems and controls activity, useful when seeking to reduce your AML organizational risk.

Of course, applying the AML brakes at key moments will be infinitely easier if you have already won over the hearts and minds of key business leaders and other stakeholders by implementing a business-focused risk control framework, as discussed in Chapter 2. Every effort will pay dividends in this area, as you need relevant managers to already know and respect you as a trusted business partner when you are giving them the message: stop now!

Client due diligence (CDD)

Formerly known as 'know your customer' or 'KYC', CDD describes the steps taken and procedures followed to gather sufficient information for an obliged entity to assess the risks that doing business with a client poses at the start of, and throughout, the client relationship.

Implementing effective CDD is a primary way of reducing organizational risk. For many financial services businesses with thousands if not millions of customers, their CDD arrangements are backed up with sophisticated software that raises 'red flags' on a risk basis to help them. The red flags, of course, are only as good as the selection criteria that raise them, and without delving into criteria selection too deeply, their critical analysis is an ongoing activity to ensure they remain effective in an ever-evolving money laundering risk environment. The very existence of a draft Fifth European Union Anti-Money Laundering Directive (5MLD) so soon after the implementation of 4MLD bears witness to this.

The purpose behind carrying out initial CDD is to know who your customers are, what they do and why they are seeking to make your organization part of their plans. Establishing beneficial ownership of funds is a key part of this: to whom does the value belong, and who stands ultimately to benefit from the relationship with your organization? In 2011, the World Bank published a report, *The Puppet Masters* (van der Does de Willebois *et al*, 2011) which examines how bribes, embezzled state assets and other criminal proceeds are being hidden via legal structures. It provides practical recommendations on how to intensify current international efforts to uncover flows of criminal money and gives compelling reasons why having effective CDD is crucial to managing customer risk. It makes interesting reading, especially if you are new to the financial crime area of compliance and want to know, 'Why do we have to spend time on gathering CDD?' CDD information generally comprises detail gathered to better understand the aspects of a client relationship, and the essentials are highlighted in the client due diligence checklist.

Client due diligence checklist

At the start of a client relationship establish the following:

- ☑ Full name/s of the client.
- ☑ Full registered entity address.
- ☑ Entity registration number.
- ☑ Nature of client business interest/occupation.
- ☑ Geographical location of client business interest/occupation.
- ☑ Rationale for/purpose of business relationship.
- ☑ Identification of the ultimate owner/s of the client entity, the beneficial owner/s.
- ☑ Are the client, beneficial owners or any relevant directors politically exposed persons (PEPs)?
- ☑ Client source of wealth.

- ☑ Client source of funds.
- ☑ Does open source online evidence back up activity declared by the client?
- ☑ Expected flow of funds business relationship set up to facilitate.
- ☑ Carry out an open sources online check with the aim of validating information given by the client and exploring whether any undeclared negative factors apply. If possible, have local language speakers and those with local knowledge also carry out checks.

During the client relationship ensure that:

- ☑ The transactions experienced match with the expected transactions of the declared business interest/occupation.
- ☑ The declared purpose of the business relationship is being fulfilled by the pattern of client activity.
- ☑ You know where the flow of funds/activity is coming from.
- ☑ You know where the flow of funds/activity is going.
- ☑ The geographical activity experienced matches the geography declared at the start of the relationship.

Stop and think

What are the CDD arrangements in your organization? Do you already gather all of the detail set out in the above checklist? If not, what needs to be added?

Although for obliged organizations CDD is required by regulation, it is also a very useful tool to introduce de-risking processes and procedures to benefit the organization as a whole. For example, CDD may reveal undeclared negative factors that the third party is keen to withhold. It may be subject to court proceedings for the recuperation of debt. It could be subject to trade sanctions under US Office of Foreign Asset Control (OFAC) or another relevant body, which makes it illegal to do business with it. Its credit rating could be very poor or it may be habitually litigious, making it a highly undesirable business partner. In both the obliged organizations and those outside of AML regulatory requirements in which I have worked, I have implemented improved CDD to minimize the risk that customers present to the organization and made improvements to corporate governance in the process. The costs avoided by implementing robust processes are difficult to quantify but the protection that effective CDD affords is a key element in reducing organizational risk. See Case Study 1.2, where Coutts & Co, a UK bank serving wealthy clients, applied weak CDD for a number of years, resulting in a fine of £8.75 million by the UK regulator.

If ever you encounter resistance to implementing improved CDD, be suspicious of the motivation behind it. Could it be laziness, where the resistant person cannot be bothered to comply with regulation? Perhaps he or she is reluctant to admit that he or she does not understand how it works and what he or she is looking for? Or, more usually, is there embarrassment at having to ask questions of the client at the start of the relationship? Worse, it could be that the success of a sales person depends upon taking higher risks and he or she does not care where the client money comes from as long as the sale results in a higher bonus. Whatever the cause of resistance to implementing CDD and perhaps all of your AML control environment, have ready all the very good reasons outside of AML regulation as to why it would be of benefit to the organization, and showcase the added value you bring in carrying out your AML work. (See Chapter 8 for further thoughts on adding value by way of cultural change and enhancing the take-up rate of policies and procedures to the benefit of your organization.)

Stop and think

List the products and services your organization is engaged in, then map them against CDD activity, current and planned, asking these questions:

1. Has the whole of your existing client base been due diligence checked, or just new clients since a certain date?
2. How regularly do you check your clients on an ongoing basis: daily, weekly, monthly, etc?
3. Do your AML controls reflect client risk profiles across the jurisdictions in which your organization operates?

Appropriate CDD differs with the type of activities the organization is engaged in, including products and services, delivery channels and geographical reach. It will help in your role as an AML professional to know the risks of your organization, and where possible to dovetail CDD carried out for AML purposes into business risk CDD. Business risk analysis may already be developed, and your diligence in knowing the risks already identified is likely to give you greater credibility when you come forward with more.

CDD for business risk could already include basic trade sanctions checking, for instance. Influencing the risk control framework could grow into an added value area that AML compliance can offer to the business if, say, a credit and litigation history check is included. Not essential for AML compliance, but useful. Make a proposal of collaboration with the business to provide combined access to CDD reports that cover the interests of AML compliance, other risk areas such as bribery, and the business risks, as far as possible, to minimize costs by carrying out checks for a number of purposes at once. This will tend to positively enhance your profile in the organization as being an engaged pro-business asset, rather than appear to be following your own AML compliance agenda that is not connected to organizational strategy or goals. Equally, your efforts to move AML compliance activity towards being an enabler, rather than generally appearing to detract from resources and the achievement of business goals, are sure to pay dividends down the line.

Enhanced due diligence

Carrying out EDD can be a fascinating exercise. On the scale of difficulty for resourcing, it is by its nature the most demanding of CDD exercises requiring considerable knowledge, attention to detail and analytical skills. It's an interesting specialism to develop. The reasons for carrying out EDD include capturing risks before they crystallize into higher-risk scenarios, such as the client being a government department located in a geography where it is known there is a high risk of corruption. The product or service may be of high value, new or little-known, perhaps delivered via new technologies. EDD processes themselves need enhanced monitoring to ensure they maintain their effectiveness in the light of emergent risks. Once analysed, the results of EDD may be useful to inform organizational strategy, as where data is gathered from EDD and mapped across to profitability, it can provide a useful link to business development modelling as a facet of risk control in harnessing opportunities.

On the financial crime front, depending on the products and services engaged in, and your AML risk assessment, appropriate EDD must be in place to minimize the risk of your organization being used as a vehicle for money laundering. High-risk factors in 4MLD that trigger the requirement for EDD are summarized below (more on the risk factors can be found in Chapter 5):

1. Customer risk
   - The customer is a PEP.
   - Operating a cash-intensive business model.
   - Holding nominee/bearer shares. These are unregistered shares, owned by the person who physically holds the share warrant.
   - Complex or unusual ownership structure.
   - Banking and operations are in different countries.
2. Product, service and delivery channel risk
   - New products and delivery channels, using new technology.
   - Anonymous products or transactions.
   - Non face-to-face transactions.
   - Private banking.
   - Payment from unknown or un-associated third parties.
3. Geography
   - Operating in high-risk countries, including the location of the entity, the supply chain and production operations.
   - Delivering products or services in high-risk countries.
   - Subject to trade sanctions.
   - Identified as having ineffective AML/CTF regimes in place by the FATF.
   - Identified as significantly corrupt by credible sources.
   - Funding and/or support offered to terrorist organizations or activities in that geography.

Once the risk assessment is complete, measures need to be established to manage those risks. Whichever industry your obliged entity belongs to, the decision to apply CDD or EDD to manage a risk will be a balancing act between cost and effectiveness, risk appetite and governance. Using the term 'proportionality' to suggest that proposed EDD activity is sufficient to control perceived risk while not being over-zealous, may be useful in making recommendations.

So, what does implementing EDD actually mean? See the list below for measures to be taken in addition to CDD that move it up to EDD. These may not appear too onerous, but each one has cost and time implications for the establishment and maintenance of the client relationship.

1 Examination of the background and/or purpose of the transaction as part of the risk assessment

Obtain additional information above that requested for standard CDD:

- Additional identity verification.
- Take additional measures to understand the:
  - background;
  - financial situation;
  - ownership of the customer;
  - supply chain or product manufacturing location.

2 Increase both the degree and the nature of monitoring of transactions

- Increase monitoring frequency.
- Check at frequent intervals that the nature and purpose of the business transaction is consistent with the declared business purpose during CDD.

Correspondent banking and reliance on third parties

Correspondent banking and reliance on third parties are called out as higher-risk activities because of the lack of direct contact the obliged entity has with the customer. A correspondent bank is one that carries out transactions and provides services on behalf of another financial institution, the respondent. Correspondent banking relationships are inherently difficult to manage as the correspondent bank has very little visibility of the activities of its customer as it is not a direct relationship, while the responsibility of EDD remains with the correspondent bank.

A key control is to prevent credit and financial firms entering into or continuing a correspondent banking relationship with a shell bank. A shell bank is one that has no physical presence in the country in which it is incorporated and which is not affiliated to any financial services group that is subject to effective, consolidated regulatory supervision. Issues with the incorporation of shell banks are high profile at the time of writing. Although shell companies have not yet been defined in law, they are generally non-trading companies set up to serve a purpose, such as making financial transactions with the benefit of anonymity. The characteristics of shell banks make them useful tools for money launderers.

Reports of criminal activity being carried out in Russia with eye-watering amounts of money being laundered by shell banks in the UK, referred to as the 'Russian laundromat', make interesting reading. The FATF clarified EDD requirements for correspondent banking and reliance upon third parties in the 2012 update of its 40 Recommendations, detailed in Table 1.1. It is its hope that by doing so, banking institutions will continue to offer correspondent relationships, which support international trade and financial inclusion. A summary of EDD measures for correspondent banking might read like this:

1. EDD measures for correspondent banks engaging with a respondent in a third country must:
   - Gather sufficient information about the respondent to understand fully the nature and purpose of its business, and assess its AML and CTF controls.
   - Carry out open-source investigation to establish the reputation of the respondent.
   - Gain approval for senior management to engage in the relationship.

2 EDD measures at the respondent bank where its customer has direct access to accounts must include:

- Checks by the respondent bank to identify and verify its customer.
- Ongoing monitoring of the customer.

This information must be provided upon request by the correspondent bank.

Politically exposed persons

PEPs are people, natural persons (as opposed to legal persons, which are incorporated entities) who, because of their activity as governmental or senior commercial officials or their affiliation with them, may be exposed to the influence of corrupt practices. They may also be likely to receive offers of benefit from assets received from corrupt practices that may be laundered through your organization, so taking enhanced measures in their screening makes sense.

The requirement to screen PEPs in local law may be only if they are foreign officials. However, in a move towards assessing the risk of all PEPs as the same, 4MLD includes domestic PEPs for the first time. It may be that a low-risk category is introduced for domestic PEPs in 5MLD that would reverse them out of the high-risk category they have just acquired, and this sort of movement is typical of the shifting nature of AML regulation.

The concept of having domestic PEPs at all brings the rationale of screening them into sharp focus. If you work for a multinational enterprise, your board of directors and chief executive officer, their families and close associates (could be) PEPs under 4MLD, and they may need to be checked as part of your due diligence.

Risk-sensitive measures must be applied to the holders of PEP-relevant domestic office in their business relationships with obliged entities until at least 12 months after they cease holding their role. Their immediate family members and close associates, where known, also come under the requirements for AML scrutiny, although in their case they are no longer deemed to be PEPs themselves as soon as the PEP they are associated with ceases to hold the office that put them into the PEP category in the first place. The PEPs below are subject to EDD under 4MLD.

- Politically exposed persons:
  - heads of state and/or of government;
  - members of high-level judicial bodies;
  - ambassadors to foreign countries;
  - directors of multinational enterprises;
  - government ministers and their deputies;
  - members of central banks;
  - senior officers of armed forces;
  - senior management and employees of state-owned enterprises.
- Immediate family members of PEPs.
- Close associates of PEPs:
  - Any natural person known to have joint beneficial ownership of commercial or other ventures.
  - Any close business relationship with a venture that is set up for the benefit of a PEP.

According to the Wolfsburg Group (2017), the rationale for including PEP screening in our EDD controls is:

> Relationships with PEPs may represent increased risks due to the possibility… (they) may misuse their power and influence for personal gain or advantage of family and close associates… they may also seek to use their power and influence to gain representation and/or access to, or control of legal entities for similar purposes.

The list of PEP roles summarized above unsurprisingly includes heads of state, heads of government, their ministers and deputies. Members of parliament or equivalent and the governing bodies of political parties are also included. These roles typically give their incumbents the authority to contract for huge national projects, and the bribes offered to these people by large multinationals hungry for contracts in construction of roads and buildings, medical and technology supplies know few bounds. See Case Study 4.1 on the extent that

Telia engaged in bribery and other corrupt practices by paying bribes to a government official. Power corrupts as they say, and absolute power corrupts absolutely. I can still see in my mind images of the thousands of pairs of shoes collected by Imelda Marcos, paid for by the proceeds of corruption when the people of the Philippines were suffering in poverty. No wonder family members and close associates of heads of state and government are included as PEPs!

CASE STUDY 4.1: Telia Company AB

The US Securities and Exchange Commission (SEC) issued a press release in September 2017 summarizing how Telia, a Sweden-based telecommunications provider, breached the Foreign Corrupt Practices Act (FCPA) by giving at least US$330 million in bribes to a family member of the President of Uzbekistan. The bribes were paid into a shell company, supposedly for lobbying and consultancy services, but these did not take place and the services were a convenient label by which to explain the bribe money. The family member was a government official with the ability to exert significant influence, and he used this to manipulate other officials to take action to the benefit of Telia. The sum put on the benefit gained by Telia for its US$330 million was US$457 million, which it had to pay in disgorgement for gains illegally made as a result of the bribery. In addition to this, Telia agreed to pay a criminal fine in excess of US$508 million, taking the whole cost of carrying out its illegal practices from 2006 to 2012 to around US$1.2 billion. Telia also agreed to implement rigorous internal controls to prevent any recurrence. The SEC worked with Dutch and Swedish authorities to bring the case against Telia, demonstrating close working relationships between FIUs and law enforcement agencies that have developed across national boundaries.

Questions

1. What internal controls exist in your organization to prevent sums being paid in bribes?
2. Do you believe that the controls are robust enough?
3. How could the financial controls of your organization be enhanced to better prevent an occurrence of bribery or other financial crime?

Members of any judicial body whose decisions are not subject to further appeal, such as supreme courts, are included as PEPs, as are members of courts of auditors and the boards of central banks. The judgement of these people can have a huge influence over the level of integrity in a jurisdiction. If the lawyers and auditors condone corruption and are laundering money themselves, the whole culture of the jurisdiction will be corrupt. Where countries are deemed at high risk of corruption on the Transparency International Corruption Index and seek to rise up the list to a less risky position, lawyers and auditors play a leading role. Where they fail, especially in countries higher up the scale (as in the case of Enron in the United States, discussed in Case Study 1.3), a significant and highly public review is likely to be undertaken which clarifies current international best practice and tolerance of corruption.

The requirement to take a risk-based approach includes implementing an assessment of the level of risk the PEP customer or beneficial owner presents to your organization. There is a distinction in 4MLD of higher- and lower-risk PEPs. The risk posed by each PEP must be assessed on a case-by-case basis, and appropriate EDD applied on a sliding scale. Once assessed, the extent of EDD to be undertaken can be decided, but whatever level of EDD is applied, senior management approval is required not only to establish a relationship with a PEP, but also to continue the relationship.

In 4MLD, 'senior management' is defined as: 'an officer or employee of the relevant person with sufficient knowledge of the relevant person's money laundering and terrorist financing risk exposure, and of sufficient authority, to take decisions affecting its risk exposure'. The term 'relevant person' as used here is a legal person as opposed to a natural person, so a legal entity rather than a living human being.

Simplified due diligence

A key change in 4MLD is the removal of a category of customers for whom SDD can be applied, resulting in the requirement for due diligence activity. There is no longer an exemption for carrying out CDD in low-risk cases, and due diligence must still be applied in cases of known low risk, including establishing the identity of the beneficial owner. Where SDD is applied, sufficient monitoring must be carried out to detect suspicious or unusual transactions. The list below provides a summary of lower-risk factors that allow SDD under Annex 2 of 4MLD:

1 Customer risk factors

- Public companies listed on a stock exchange and subject to disclosure requirements, which include adequate transparency of beneficial ownership.
- Public administrations or enterprises.
- Customers resident in geographical areas of lower risk.

2 Product, service, transaction or delivery channel risk factors

- Life insurance policies for which the premium is assessed as low.
- Insurance policies for pension schemes if there is no early surrender option and the policy cannot be used as collateral.
- A pension, superannuation or similar scheme that provides retirement benefits to employees, where contributions are made by way of deduction from wages, and the scheme rules do not permit the assignment of a member's interest under the scheme.
- Financial products or services that provide limited services to certain types of customers, to increase the access to financial services to customers who otherwise would not be able to benefit from them.
- Products where the risks of money laundering and terrorist financing are managed by other factors such as purse limits in some types or electronic money, or transparency of ownership.

3 Geographical risk factors

- Member States within the European Union (EU).
- Third countries (countries outside of the EU) having effective AML/CTF systems.
- Third countries identified by credible sources as having a low level of corruption or other criminal activity.

- Third countries which, on the basis of credible sources such as FATF mutual evaluations, have requirements to combat money laundering and terrorist financing consistent with the revised FATF Recommendations and effectively implement those requirements.

Summary of notable changes in 4MLD

The various changes in 4MLD, discussed separately and in more detail elsewhere in the book, are summarized below to give you an overview of where changes may need to be implemented to the AML control framework in your organization to bring it into compliance.

> **Stop and think**
>
> Would you have to enhance your current due diligence processes to comply with known AML requirements such as those in 4MLD? Use the summary lists below as reference.

1 Beneficial ownership

- *Companies:* No major changes, beneficial ownership threshold still at 25 per cent ownership, or otherwise exercising control.
- *Trusts:*
  - Increase of scope from those beneficiaries with an interest of >25 per cent to all beneficiaries.
  - Where the beneficial owner is a class of persons who may benefit from the trust, as defined in the UK Joint Money Laundering Steering Group Guidance Part 1, Paragraph 5.3.16, the name and scope of the class only is necessary, and not the names of every member of the class.
  - CDD must be carried out on the settlor of a trust. The settlor is the person who establishes and puts assets into a trust, and decides how the assets in a trust should be used, by way of a trust deed.

- CDD must also be carried out on the trustee, who carries out the wishes of the settlor, managing the trust on a day-to-day basis.
- Finally, CDD must be carried out on any other person who exercises control over a trust and its assets.

2 Scope increase

The scope of money laundering regulation has increased to cover:

- Dealers in high-value goods, for cash payments greater than €10,000 (€15,000 under 3MLD).
- Providers of gambling services, including casinos that were caught under 3MLD.
- Independent legal professionals.
- Trust or company service providers.
- Estate agents, including letting agents where applicable.

3 Clarification of which businesses are deemed to be doing business in the UK

Obliged entities with registered office/head office in the UK whether managing the business in the UK or passporting into the EU.

4 AML/CTF policies and procedures for all obliged entities

Ensure that AML/CTF policies and procedures apply for all group companies, including subsidiaries and branches. Share information on AML/CTF across group companies, in compliance with data privacy regulation.

5 Local law being contrary to 4MLD

Where local law does not permit the implementation of 4MLD, inform the relevant regulator:

- Implement enhanced risk-mitigation measures.
- Regulator has the authority to direct the entity to cease transaction types, relationships or business.

6 Risk-based approach

Obliged entity risk assessments must be documented, up-to-date and available to regulators upon request. Taking into account the size and nature of the business, there must be risk assessments against the following factors:

- customer type;
- country or geographic area;
- product or service type;
- delivery channel;
- transaction type.

7 Policies

Policies must be a written record, approved by senior management. They must be proportionate to the size and nature of the organization, and include:

- Risk management practices; the identification and scrutiny of complex/unusual transactions with no apparent purpose; and measures to mitigate risks of using new technology.
- Internal controls.
- Client Due Diligence.
- Reporting, record-keeping and monitoring.
- Internal communication.

8 Internal controls

Governance controls covering the areas of:

- Internal audit.
- New hires screening.
- Appointment of a responsible officer at board or senior management level.

9 Training

Training must be given to:

- Relevant employees, on relevant subjects to include AML/CTF awareness and data privacy laws.

- Enable employees to recognize suspicious activity, and have awareness of the tools available to deal with instances when they arise.

10 Customer Due Diligence for financial services organizations

The requirement for CDD is triggered:

- At the establishment of a business relationship.
- When carrying out an occasional transaction greater than €15,000, and where a transaction constitutes a transfer of funds under the Funds Transfer Regulations of more than €1,000.
- Where suspicion of money laundering or terrorist financing occurs, including with authenticity of evidence provided.
- CDD for existing customers to take place on a risk-sensitive basis when appropriate and/or where the circumstances of a customer change that have an impact upon the relevant risk assessment.

11 Customer Due Diligence identification and verification of customer

CDD information to be gathered at the start of a business relationship:

- Identification and verification. This typically consists of a government-issued photo-identity, plus proof of address via utility bill or similar received by the customer within a limited recent timeframe.
- Gather and assess information on the intended purpose of the relationship, and its nature.
- In the case of companies, obtain and verify:
  - full company name;
  - address of registered office;
  - company registration number;
  - principal place of business;
  - applicable law;
  - names of registered company directors.

- If the customer is beneficially owned by another person (apart from listed companies):
  - Identify and take reasonable measures to verify the beneficial owner, and understand the nature of ownership.
  - Where it is not possible to identify the beneficial owner, keep records of the most senior person identified for the purposes of beneficial ownership verification.
  - Record the identity of and verify the person who claims to act for the customer, and verify their authority to act.

12 Customer Due Diligence and the relevance of risk assessment

This regulation sets out the elements that must be taken into account when carrying out CDD in line with the risk assessment of the customer. When assessing the level of risk that a customer relationship presents, the organization must include:

- The purpose of the business relationship, account or transaction.
- The amounts of money involved. The larger the amount of assets or funds being transferred, the greater the risk of money laundering.
- The duration of the business relationship and frequency of activity within it.

The firm must be able to demonstrate that it has taken appropriate CDD measures in managing the risks to which the business relationship exposes the firm.

13 Timing of Customer Due Diligence

The default timing of CDD remains: at the start of the business relationship, before it is established; when the customer is carrying out a relevant occasional transaction.

14 Enhanced Due Diligence

Where EDD is required, the firm must:

- Examine the background and/or purpose of the transaction as part of its assessment.

- Increase both the degree and the nature of monitoring of transactions.
- Where EDD is required, the firm may include:
  - obtaining additional identity verification;
  - taking additional measures to understand the background, financial situation and ownership of the customer;
  - checking that the nature and purpose of the business transaction is consistent with the declared business purpose during CDD;
  - increased monitoring.

15 Enhanced Due Diligence – high-risk factors

- Customers:
  - Operating in high-risk countries.
  - Cash intensive business model.
  - Holding nominee/bearer shares. These are unregistered shares, owned by the person who physically holds the share warrant.
  - Complex or unusual ownership structure.
- Product, service and delivery channel:
  - New products and delivery channels, using new technology.
  - Anonymous products or transactions.
  - Private banking.
  - Payment from unknown or un-associated third parties.
  - Non face-to-face transactions.
- Geography:
  - Subject to trade sanctions.
  - Identified as having ineffective AML/CTF regimes in place.
  - Identified as significantly corrupt by credible sources.
  - Funding and/or support offered to terrorist organizations or activities in that geography.

16 Enhanced Due Diligence – correspondent relationships

EDD for correspondent banks engaging with a respondent in a third country must:

- Gather sufficient information about the respondent to understand fully the nature and purpose of its business, and assess its AML and CTF controls.
- Carry out open-source investigation to establish the reputation of the respondent.
- Gain approval for senior management to engage in the relationship.

Where the respondent bank's customer has direct access to accounts, the EDD must include checks by the respondent bank to identify and verify its customer and carry out ongoing checks. This information must be provided upon request by the correspondent bank.

17 Enhanced Due Diligence – politically exposed persons

PEPs are people who hold or have held a prominent public role in the last 12 months, their immediate family members and known close associates:

- Scope of a PEP increased to include beneficial owners.
- Domestic PEPs as well as foreign PEPs included.
- Risk-sensitive measures must be applied to business relationships with PEPs until at least 12 months after they cease holding the public role, or until they are assessed not to pose a risk.
- Immediate family members and known close associates can cease to be deemed a PEP immediately public office is relinquished.

The list of PEP roles includes:

- Heads of state, heads of government, ministers and deputy or assistant ministers.
- Members of parliament or of similar legislative bodies.
- Members of the governing bodies of political parties.
- Members of supreme courts, of constitutional courts or of any judicial body the decisions of which are not subject to further appeal other than in exceptional circumstances.
- Members of courts of auditors or of the boards of central banks.
- Ambassadors, *charges d'affaires* and high-ranking officers in the armed forces.

- Members of the administrative, management or supervisory bodies of state-owned enterprises.
- Directors, deputy directors and members of the board or equivalent function of an international organization.

Establish before pay-out of life assurance policies whether the beneficiary is a PEP, and in higher-risk cases scrutinize the entire relationship with the policyholder and inform senior management before pay-out. There is a distinction in 4MLD of higher- and lower-risk PEPs. The risk posed by each PEP must be assessed on a case-by-case basis, and appropriate EDD applied on a sliding scale.

18 Simplified Due Diligence

A key change in 4MLD is the removal of a category of customers for whom SDD can be applied. There is no longer an exemption for carrying out CDD in low-risk cases, and due diligence must still be applied in cases of known low risk, including establishing the identity of the beneficial owner. Where SDD is applied, sufficient monitoring must be carried out to detect suspicious or unusual transactions.

19 Reliance on third parties for CDD

Reliance on a third party to carry out CDD is allowed under 4MLD where the third party is a 'relevant person' subject to 4MLD or equivalent themselves:

- Responsibility for CDD rests with the relying firm, including the identity of the customer or beneficial owner.
- Ensuring that the CDD is suitable also rests with the relying firm, which remains liable for failures in compliance.
- A new record-keeping requirement includes the production upon request of customer or beneficial owner verification.

20 Record keeping and data protection

CDD and transaction records must be kept for a minimum of five years and a maximum of 10 years after the transaction takes place or the relationship comes to an end. After that time personal records must be deleted, and express consent of the data subject is required to keep them for a longer period. Personal data may only be used for the purposes of the business relationship, and not for other purposes.

Note: there is a tension between the requirements of 4MLD and those of the General Data Privacy Regulation (GDPR). Although the GDPR includes increased financial penalties for non-compliance, violations of 4MLD have criminal consequences, so it may be wise to err on compliance with 4MLD rather than the GDPR should you have to deal with a conflict of their application.

Key takeaways

- Clarity on correspondent banking provided by the FATF revision of its 40 Recommendations as adopted in 2012 is included in 4MLD. FATF hopes that the increased clarity will encourage banks to maintain their correspondent banking arrangements, rather than to de-risk their operations by ceasing to engage in them.
- The distinction between foreign and domestic PEPs is removed in 4MLD, increasing the burden of AML activity for obliged entities.
- There is no longer an exemption to carrying out CDD checks on classes of customers assessed as low risk.
- When considering record keeping requirements for 4MLD against the requirements of the GDPR, be aware that failures in 4MLD may have criminal consequences for individuals, and GDPR failures do not.

References and further reading

Department of Justice (2017) Telia Company AB and its Uzbek Subsidiary Enter into a Global Foreign Bribery Resolution of More Than $965 Million for Corrupt Payments in Uzbekistan, Justice News 21/9, available from: www.justice.gov/opa/pr/telia-company-ab-and-its-uzbek-subsidiary-enter-global-foreign-bribery-resolution-more-965 (last accessed 2 February 2018)

Directive (EU) 2015/849 of the European Parliament and of The Council of 20 May 2015 on the prevention of the use of the financial system for the purposes of money laundering or terrorist financing, amending Regulation (EU) No 648/2012 of the European Parliament and of the Council, and repealing Directive 2005/60/EC of the European

Parliament and of the Council and Commission Directive 2006/70/EC (Fourth Money Laundering Directive)
Hudson, D and Judareh, K (2017) *Implementing 4MLD: The new AML/CTF regime*, Herbert Smith Freehills, London
Office of Foreign Asset Control website: www.treasury.gov/resource-center/sanctions/Pages/default.aspx
United States v Telia Company AB (2017) Docket No. 17-CR-581-GBD
van der Does de Willebois, E, Halter, E M, Harrison, R A, Park, Ji Won, Sharman, J C (2011) *The Puppet Masters. How the corrupt use legal structures to hide stolen assets and what to do about it. Stolen asset recovery initiative*, The World Bank, available at: https://star.worldbank.org/star/sites/star/files/puppetmastersv1.pdf (last accessed 23 January 2018)
The Wolfsberg Group (2017) Wolfsberg Guidance on Politically Exposed Persons (PEPs), available from: http://www.wolfsberg-principles.com/pdf/standards/Wolfsberg-Guidance-on-PEPs-May-2017.pdf (last accessed 14 February 2018)

Country and people risk

05

Having an effective anti-money laundering (AML) risk management framework includes the thorough identification of risks known to exist in the organization, then gaining sufficient data from management information produced by the controls of those risks to serve you well by ensuring that your organization is not a desirable place for criminals to launder the proceeds of their crimes.

Assessment of risks in an organization and mapping policies, procedures and controls around them depends on having an overall appreciation of those risks to start with. In this chapter we will explore some of the main aspects to consider when implementing AML risk controls in your organization.

This chapter covers:

- Applying a risk-based approach.
- Country risk.
- People risk.
- Knowledge gaps.
- Assumptions that encourage reduced diligence.

Applying a risk-based approach

So, what is meant by 'applying a risk-based approach?' First, it means identifying the risks associated with an activity, in this case the transactional arrangements of your organization. It's all about finding where the value is and exploring the controls on movement of the value to manage its integrity and purpose.

Application of a risk-based approach should always take into consideration the unknown as well as known risks to provide flexibility in the risk management process. While serving as Defense Secretary to George W Bush, Donald Rumsfeld made a statement about known and unknown risks that has been used as shorthand for organizational risk management, illustrated in Figure 5.1. Rumsfeld's point was that decisions can be made about risks and their management that are proven totally wrong in reality because of assumptions made with insufficient knowledge. He was categorizing risks in a way that demonstrates one can never be sure that every risk is covered, and the relevance to reducing AML risk in your organization is that providing flexibility to accommodate the unknowns is a key element of sound risk management.

Having the AML regulatory requirement to apply a risk-based approach gives organizations the authority to identify and assess the risk factors peculiar to their own environment. The identification of organizational risks together with current regulatory risks, such as introduced by the Fourth European Union Anti-Money Laundering Directive (4MLD) identified in Chapter 4, provides a risk universe. Risk mitigation can then be applied, leaving your organization with inevitable residual risks that need to be managed, and mitigation

Figure 5.1 Known and unknown risks

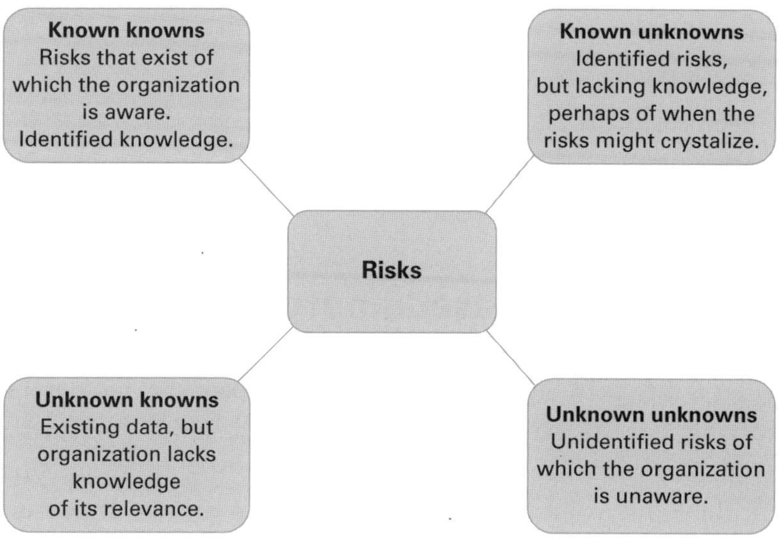

factors that require monitoring and updating. Using the AML strategy wheel identified in Chapter 3 can help you with this. Then, with a risk assessment in place, allocation of limited resources can be given to the management of higher-risk areas, with areas of lower risk still managed but in a way that consumes less resource.

How do people in the organization know about their role in managing risks? That all comes down to engendering staff awareness, which is where training and communication come in, as discussed in Chapter 2. Once they appreciate the money laundering risk related to their role, employees become active resources in reducing organizational risk. Together with procedural training specific to their role, employees become aware of the changing risk environment, what to look for and how to deal with it. With this knowledge they are empowered to take responsibility and act to prevent money laundering happening in their organization. The 'what' of what to do in the role to identify and manage AML risk comes together with the 'how' of how risk management empowerment is enabled to form an effective AML risk control environment, by way of greater understanding.

Organizational risks extend beyond those for AML, of course, and in my experience nothing is better at turning away the minds of business leaders from their AML responsibilities than AML Compliance only recognizing the risks they are concerned with, and not placing them within the wider commercial and financial risks that business leaders have to manage on a daily basis. So, seek to map AML risks into an existing business-wide risk matrix if that is possible.

When thinking about managing your AML risks, it may be helpful to use imagery such as in Figure 5.2, and use it as shorthand to explain your activities throughout the organization. Developing a core explanatory presentation of the AML risks to be managed for senior function leaders and their teams provides a consistent message. Weave them into the strategic goals of your organization for added impact. It may not be necessary or appropriate to actually deliver the presentation, but developing it will help you to articulate AML risk management more readily and help your proposals spring to mind should the opportunity arise to share them. Perhaps you could draft it for your nominated AML Officer? In any event, it will be useful research of your organization's risk universe with which

Figure 5.2 Visual risk mapping

to wow your manager, demonstrating your appreciation of AML and your knowledge of your organization. In communicating your AML risk strategy to leaders and subject-matter experts in the legal, commercial, financial and regulatory areas, be sure to highlight the connections to their areas of responsibility so as to hold their attention, and to focus their minds on the subject of your AML control 'ask'. The factors to consider in your AML risk-based approach are summarized in the checklists below. These factors are discussed in this chapter and in Chapter 6.

AML risk assessment: factors

In your AML risk assessment, include the following factors, taking into account the size and nature of your business:

- customer type;
- country or geographic area;
- product or service type;
- delivery channel;
- transaction type.

AML risk assessment: auditable records

Obliged-entity risk assessments must be:

- documented;
- up to date; and
- available to regulators upon request.

Country risk

As discussed in Chapter 2, for multinational organizations country risk features large in assessing the risks of doing business. Wherever in the world you and your organization are based, your perception of country risk is likely to be coloured by the local custom and practice that you and your peers perceive as normal. Because of this it is essential for AML compliance purposes to reach out to the international bodies of the Financial Action Task Force (FATF), the Wolfsberg Group and others to calibrate your views on what risks are prevalent in your jurisdiction (see Chapter 1 for more details). This necessity may not be evident even to those who are providing training to prospective AML professionals!

CASE STUDY 5.1: Culture v AML norms

At the time when the Greek government was encouraging activity in the housing market by accepting cash payments for houses with no questions asked, a lecturer at a London university was on sick leave during a series of scheduled AML lectures to a postgraduate class of students from 11 different countries. To cover the classes, a replacement was quickly found at another university close by. The replacement was a Greek national with an out-of-date presentation giving the names of government departments from a previous era, and with views to match. He gave a brief lecture on financial crime and then set the class a task to establish all of the reasons why tax evasion is of lesser concern than other types of criminal activity, and can, for all intents and purposes, be removed from consideration when carrying out AML checking. All of the students who did not have a financial services background prepared their rationale using the lecture and their local country norms to inform their response. Argentina, Canada, France, Nigeria, Pakistan and the UK were among those represented. The only AML Responsible Officer (RO) in the room was alarmed that the lecturer was misguiding his students and strongly countered the premise, arguing that spending the profits from the criminal activity of tax evasion, even on buying a house no questions asked, is actually money laundering. This led to an uncomfortably surprised lecturer, but a good debate.

Questions

1. Does your culture operate a cash economy? Bear in mind the checks and balances required by FATF when assessing the work needed to achieve AML compliance in your organization.
2. When you deliver AML training, does your audience listen and ask constructive questions, or do they blandly sit through it, ignoring its content?
3. Are you a lone AML voice in your organization? See if you can find a group of AML ROs you can join to provide balance of expectation in your AML control environment.

Case Study 5.1 illustrates that, as well as the need for universities to screen lecturers before letting them loose on their students, cultural norms can override the knowledge of regulation and its requirements, on the basis of, 'If it is happening in my country it must be ok.' The natural drive for keeping to the culture we know, which sometimes results in quite elaborate justifications to avoid accepting change, can misinform one's own perceptions and influence the perceptions of others. Correcting this by reference to current international AML regulatory developments and the country in which you are applying them will help to guide your organization in implementing a relevant control framework that works across national boundaries.

To illustrate another facet of country risk, see Case Study 5.2. Where there is little awareness of what to expect from financial investments, criminals can use relatively simple deceptions to acquire money, and the services of easily accessible organizations for money laundering until law enforcement decides to take action. In Case Study 5.2, it is the fraudster preying on the trust and inexperience of his countrymen, offering them high returns for little investment, that gives rise to the money laundering.

CASE STUDY 5.2: Financial awareness

For the first time in the country's history, in April 2017 a 63-year-old Bruneian man, Pengiran Hussin bin Pengiran Sulaiman, was jailed for offences relating to running a fake investment scheme and money laundering, including misleading investors. As reported in the *Borneo Bulletin*, the defendant met a victim in a restaurant and informed him that he would have to pay B$6,350 to participate in the investment scheme and as a return on this he would receive:

- a Mercedes Benz S280 car;
- B$200,000 in cash;
- B$60,000 in cash every month for life;
- a house valued at B$400,000;
- a Rolex watch;
- a trip to perform Haj pilgrimage;
- a VIP Global Card allowing the holder to withdraw up to $200,000 from any ATM in the world.

Believing the defendant, the victim handed over the money to him (Faisal, 2017).

Once victims found that they were not receiving the payments as described by Sulaiman, several of them complained to the police and he was arrested. The Commercial Crime Investigations Division of the Royal Brunei Police Force discovered that the defendant conned a total of B$147,581 out of several victims of the fake investment scheme, some of whom he enticed by claiming it was a charitable programme, Amal Jariah. The defendant committed money laundering when he transferred the amount he collected via Western Union to an accomplice in the Philippines.

Questions

1. Do you believe that people in your jurisdiction are relatively financially aware, or naïve?
2. What is the normal way that investment products are marketed in your jurisdiction – personal approach by individuals based on trust, or by regulated corporate entities?

In Case Study 5.2, one might be tempted to comment on the ridiculous level of return offered with 'If it sounds too good to be true, it usually is.' However, these are clearly naïve investors trusting in the manager of the supposed investment scheme to pay out in line with his promises. Where were the AML regulatory players in Borneo, and why did the investors not see the fraud? Where AML regulation and financial awareness are developed, more sophisticated schemes are required to dupe investors, such as the Ponzi scheme Bernard Madoff created (see Case Study 5.5). On reviewing the Transparency International Corruption Perceptions Index 2016 to see what sort of position Borneo is on the list, I noted three records of the territories that make up Borneo: Brunei at 41, Malaysia at 55 and Indonesia is at 90 out of the 176 countries, those with the least perceived corruption having the lower numbers. Brunei, where the money launderer in Case Study 5.2 came from, is listed as least corrupt.

In de-risking your organization note that local culture and the level of financial sophistication and awareness of financial crime can exponentially increase the risks you face in operating in those geographies. Your AML and anti-bribery and corruption controls need to acknowledge this point, using your country risk matrix as reference. You will have country, people, product and delivery channel risks to map together in it. If you use the country risk as a basic guide to the awareness of financial crime and money laundering among local people, you will have created a sound basis for your risk matrix. Application of controls after your risk assessment will include enhanced due diligence appropriate to the perceived risk in each of the countries in which your organization carries out activities.

People risk

People risk is as relevant within the organization as it is externally. Considering external risks first, your organization is at greater customer risk where operating in high-risk countries, as above, and where it provides higher-risk services to customers including those with a cash-intensive or non face-to-face service. The internet has enabled the proliferation of non face-to-face services that can be delivered very quickly, and developing controls to reduce cybercrime has created a whole new industry, as discussed in Chapter 6.

For AML purposes, client due diligence is the main method used to mitigate the people risk coming from outside the organization, as discussed in Chapter 4. That leaves people risk coming from inside an organization, which can manifest itself in several ways. To err is human, and beyond that, the risk of your organization being used by rogue employees as a vehicle for financial crime and money laundering can be increased by:

- Lack of employee training together with proof of competence; see Chapter 3.
- Deliberate lack of adherence to policies and procedures. This is an area for liaison with HR.
- Poor management tracking of AML controls. Ensure your data management controls are in place to provide tracking and monitoring of AML data for relevant managers.
- Pushing for expediency and results. This is the risk/reward dichotomy for commercial leadership. It is possible to push employees into non-compliance with relevant laws by offering them excessive rewards for achieving high sales goals. These incentives can encourage a higher-risk attitude from employees and result in unintended criminal consequences.

All of these areas are the focus of AML professionals, and data gathered from employee training is key to proving that they have the necessary knowledge to comply with relevant laws. Lack of proven employee training and competence can lead to criminal consequences for the AML RO in some jurisdictions, which surely focuses the mind (see Chapter 6 for more). Online training enables auditable records to be gathered automatically by learning management software, and it provides AML ROs with valuable proof of mitigating this known risk. One can never fully ensure employee competence, but what you can do, as shown in Case Study 2.2, is to evidence that you have taken all reasonable and proportionate steps to prevent corruption within your organization, and that matters.

In my experience, the time it takes to tailor AML training for an organization is far outweighed by the benefits it affords to the de-risking of processes, and the potential time and resource saved by better educated employees staying on track and producing fewer crystallized risks in their work. Even with this knowledge in place, there can be a certain amount of courage required by AML professionals when employees choose not to know. Consider Case Study 5.3 involving a manager of an insurance company with global reach, an architect of non-compliance, with attitude.

CASE STUDY 5.3: Aggravated non-compliance

A consultancy organization based in the United States secured a contract to establish an insurance solution for a prestigious film maker, to be effective in all countries where it had studios and carried out filming. Although Sergio, the contracting manager, knew that there were most probably insurance licence requirements and restrictions in the relevant countries, he decided it would be more expedient to sign the contract and keep well away from Legal and Compliance policies. Contract signed, he set to work in the first 20 countries. No licences were in place. Thinking he could weave around regulatory requirements and company policy, in his next meeting with AML RO Alison, Sergio had some commercially sound patter rehearsed. Alison had good company intelligence herself. She already knew the contract was in place, and that the client due diligence (CDD) process had not been followed, so she asked Sergio for evidence of the CDD to call him out. Discovered in wrongdoing, Sergio came out fighting, and he used his own non-compliance to accuse Alison of negligence.

Although shocked at Sergio's response, Alison managed to stay composed and reiterated that CDD, including a review of local country laws and licence requirements, would have to be carried out. She fully expected what happened next, and was at her desk really early the next day, coffee in hand, waiting for Sergio's attempt to shift the blame for his non-compliance to her. Within minutes Alison received a scathing e-mail from Sergio, copying her manager and, prepared, she was able to respond very quickly with exactly the purpose of her request and the activities required by the laws of the countries in question. Sergio had escalated his wrongdoing to precisely the person to strengthen the case against him. Legal and HR engagement followed, and when Sergio was summoned to explain himself his response was simply perfect for a bully under the spotlight. He shrugged his shoulders and admitted that avoiding process was part of his usual modus operandi of taking a strong approach in business dealings. If he was found out avoiding Legal and Compliance, he justified his actions by stating that Legal and Compliance had not taken the time to give him the advice he needed. On this occasion it resulted in a reality check for Sergio, who was instructed to moderate his behaviour and ensure that all future contracts followed company policy and process. In collaboration with Internal Audit and Sergio's manager, Alison then began a comprehensive review of the contract and associated matters.

Sergio was choosing not to know the compliant path and created loopholes in established processes to go rogue. Being a senior manager with bullish behaviour, it took courage to challenge his actions. What was in it for him? Questions had to be asked!

Questions

1 How did Sergio win the contract? Did he pay a bribe to win it, or receive a kick-back?
2 Did Sergio offer any incentives to government officials or commercial organizations when establishing the insurance in each country?
3 Was the contracting party subject to any trade sanctions or AML restrictions that the organization may be violating by doing business with them?
4 What commercial pressures were being placed on Sergio to drive his behaviour?
5 What company incentives were being offered to Sergio to drive his behaviour?
6 Why had Sergio's non-compliance to policy not been noticed before?
7 Could Sergio's AML training record be proven in the event of investigation by external parties?
8 How could the contracting process be improved to prevent a reoccurrence?
9 What senior management messages were being given and how might these be strengthened to improve the AML control environment?

When delinquency is found, finding answers to questions such as those in Case Study 5.3 is necessary to drive AML compliance and perhaps enhance the AML control environment. If no action is taken, bullish behaviour and non-compliance to policy is likely to spread through the organization. Carpe diem, and use challenging opportunities to drive the AML de-risking agenda by reducing known risks.

People risk in the form of bullying of AML professionals by colleagues resisting improved systems and controls is the reality that must occasionally be lived through, so before taking an AML role, carry out your own due diligence on the recruiting employer. At an interview for a joint Compliance Officer/Money Laundering Reporting Officer role at a building society in middle England, I found that the new incumbent would be placed between Marketing, who were bringing new higher-risk products to market, and Legal, who opposed the changed product portfolio. The Compliance Officer would earn half as much as either of his or her peers on the Marketing and Legal sides, and in my view was being placed as a disadvantaged buffer between two warring factions. I withdrew my application for the post. This sort of scenario can play out in all the governance functions, including legal, finance and company secretariat. Consider the case of Michael Woodford, former Chief Executive Officer (CEO) of Japan-based manufacturer, Olympus Corporation, in Case Study 5.4.

CASE STUDY 5.4: Michael Woodford

Michael Woodford joined Olympus in 1981, and by 2011 had risen from managing its European operations to becoming CEO of the whole organization, the first non-Japanese person to hold the position. As CEO, he gained access to the company financial records, and very soon recognized that something was wrong. Using hierarchical command authority, still-powerful former CEO, Tsuyoshi Kikukawa, and deputy president, Hisashi Mori tried to prevent him questioning $687 million fees for merger and acquisition (M&A) advice on the purchase of three 'Mickey Mouse' companies at a cost of almost £1 billion. Woodford recognized that the costs associated with this deal were enormous: 'It was the largest payment ever made for M&A advice in the history of capitalism by a factor of three.' He blew the whistle on Olympus, exposing the largest loss-concealing financial crimes in Japan's corporate history. The companies paid for M&A work appeared to have connections to organized crime groups, and Woodford, understanding that his life may be in danger, flew out of Tokyo to London. The scandal led to the resignation of the whole Olympus board of directors, and the investigation that followed included its auditor and bankers. After a very uncomfortable time at the centre of this scandal, Woodford was recognized for his bravery in exposing the corporate financial crimes and eventually received a pay-out from Olympus for severance of his contract.

Question

1 Having worked for Olympus for 30 years, one might assume that Michael Woodford would know already that there were issues with its costs for mergers and acquisitions. Clearly not! Does your organization have a culture of hierarchy and obedience to senior management? Transparency of financial control activity to relevant parties is key to maintaining integrity of reporting and risk management.

Against the people risk of one's own colleagues and known risks hidden by senior management, customer risk may seem quite pedestrian, but it plays a large part in controlling the financial crime and money laundering risk of the organization. For more on customer risk, see Chapter 4.

Knowledge gaps

In an ideal world from a *criminal perspective*, money launderers can benefit from the AML knowledge gaps in your organization. They can either commit a crime and use their goods or money straight away without any CDD checks being made on their transactions, or receive funds in recompense for their part in a fraud, robbery or other criminal act, and again just spend and enjoy. In an ideal world from an *AML perspective*, there would be no gaps in knowledge: all risks would be known and mitigated. The criminal and money launderer would not be able to benefit safely from their crimes, everyone would be aware and alert for money laundering prevention, and automated alert systems would catch suspect transactions every time. It is we AML professionals who have to mind the gap between one ideal world and the other.

Every day bright, innovative criminals are developing strategies and new ways to launder the proceeds of their crimes, producing new and as yet unknown risks with which to test your organization's controls. Because of this, in my view a good AML starting mind-set is to have every respect for criminal ingenuity and work ethic, albeit driven by greed. As AML professionals, we have a lot to live up to in staying ahead, and when the amount of time that you can afford to spend on gap analysis during your busy working day is taken into consideration, it is no wonder that the balance of creative energy is very much in favour of success by the money launderer. This is why we need flexibility in our AML risk control environment, to adapt quickly to previously unknown risks. We need vigilance in our colleagues as well as ourselves, to spot the signs, the red flags denoting money laundering and fraud that may appear when engaging with elements both inside and outside our organizations. You can be sure that, should your organization or products be targeted, the money launderer will have all of their attention focused on the ways in which weaknesses can be exploited, if possible without you even noticing.

In acknowledgement of this, I always consider there are gaps in AML controls that have just not been noticed yet. This stance keeps me looking for the gaps, and asking questions of the AML controls in place. Although unlikely to be sufficient to plug all the gaps as there are always the unknown unknowns, this stance helps AML professionals to combat the continual tendency for criminals to find new ways to commit fraud and potentially find weaknesses in AML control environments. This criminal tendency is exacerbated by developments in technology and cybercrime that help them. It is also helped by trained people in your organization, who know what your policies require, making assumptions that discourage awareness and due diligence.

Assumptions that encourage reduced diligence

Trust

Trust between parties is a major factor in discouraging due diligence. It may be that one of your senior managers is a lifelong friend of the owner of a company that is about to start a business relationship with your organization. 'Do not embarrass me by asking him for identification and verification,' may come the cry. Red flag! Transparency is one of the pillars of good governance, and CDD has become familiar to those in jurisdictions with AML regulatory requirements. Acceptance or otherwise of verifying identity in compliance with AML regulation is a clear indication of the type of business relationship desired by the third party. The effectiveness of your AML policy, guidance and controls will be tested in this scenario. Can senior managers push through the establishment of the business relationship without completing CDD? If they can, you are not receiving appropriate leadership from your senior management as they are introducing unknown AML risks to your organization.

Gaining respectability and building trust in order to deceive others may be a lifetime's work by the criminal, preying on individuals to hand over their money once they have drawn them into their confidence. Consider the efforts of Bernard Madoff in Case Study 5.5, who became a trusted and very wealthy investment adviser, a highly respected person who created an empire of luxury for his family using other people's money.

CASE STUDY 5.5: Bernard Madoff

Bernard Madoff was a self-made businessman who, as a child growing up in modest circumstances, saw his father's business fail and become bankrupt. He started his own brokerage business in 1960 with his father-in-law's help and claimed that it grew as a bona fide business until 1992, when he began his descent into fraud. Growing in confidence as the fraudulent business flourished, his business became the largest Ponzi scheme of all time. At the same time, Madoff's bullying of his work colleagues increased, so that no one dared to challenge him.

The Madoff scheme grew while he was vice-chairman of the US industry watchdog, the National Association of Securities Dealers, but he deceived the regulator, banks, investors and his own family members into believing he ran a highly successful investment scheme while syphoning off large sums of money. This worked while there was more coming in to be invested than the amount being taken out, as Madoff started to pay off long-term investors with money from new entrants. All the time he was using money in the scheme to fund a lavish lifestyle for himself and his family, with luxury houses and yachts around the world. It has been reported that the theft amounted to US$17.5 billion from more than 4,000 investors, the largest Ponzi scheme in history. Madoff laundered the money stolen from the scheme by paying for the luxury items for himself and his family. With his high profile and position of trust, no one during the entire 10 years of the scheme challenged him or saw through to his criminality.

Questions

1. Are there any very well respected executives in your organization who appear to be unaware of your AML systems and controls?
2. Do any of these executives impose a culture of fear in the organization?
3. What sort of whistleblowing arrangements do you have for reporting wrongdoing by senior executives?
4. What is the likelihood that one of your own executives could be using your organization to commit fraud or launder the proceeds of crime?

Note: Ponzi schemes

A Ponzi scheme is a type of scam where unsophisticated investors are wooed by promises of large returns on their investment in a short timescale. Initial investors are paid from the funds of new investors, so the scheme appears to perform extremely well, with very little risk. However, when the cash outflow exceeds cash inflow the scheme collapses, as the money has already been paid away to earlier investors. Charles Ponzi's inventive scheme brought in more than US$15 million in the year before his arrest in 1920, but he only ever purchased around US$30 worth of the mail coupons underpinning the scheme.

Habit

Habit also is a driving force for reducing the attention to detail in questioning why an arrangement is in place. In shipping, gifts to the harbour master or port authorities are sometimes common place and an important part of the sequence of events when vessels enter a new port, especially where there is a perishable cargo on board. Expected by both the giver and receiver, arrangements for the ship's docking and services rendered may include giving alcohol or a 'donation to the pension fund' whereas it is in reality a facilitation payment, to persuade a government official to carry out the work that can legally be expected to be fulfilled without payment. Perhaps a little closer to home for our obliged entities, consider the scenario in Case Study 5.6.

CASE STUDY 5.6: Facilitation payments

The Cairo location of a global company with its head office in London was outside of the central business district, along the road towards Sphinx International Airport. Good for travel connections, certainly, but it was quite a walk for the postman, who was sometimes late with his deliveries or missed them altogether.

Sales director Jazeb was expecting an urgent delivery of a signed document, giving him the go-ahead to start working on a project with tight timescales. He asked Ammon, the office manager, when the post would be delivered that day. Ammon's response was that the postal delivery would be fine because, now he had authority over petty cash payments, he would make sure the postman received his 'usual encouragement' to deliver in good time. Ammon would book it as 'sundry items' and, as the amounts were so small, they would not draw the attention of Finance or Internal Audit. Although happy that he would receive his signed document, Jazeb had completed his AML compliance training only the previous week, and knew the rights and wrongs of cash payments. Jazeb queried the practice using the company's AML compliance mailbox and in the following weeks he noted the management move towards electronic signatures for key documents, and Ammon's complaint about new constraints on cash payments. The postman was used to receiving payments for carrying out his duties, and Ammon was used to those requests. In his case the company training did not override local custom and practice. Jazeb was able to confidently report the practice of facilitation payments being made, and AML Compliance were able to bring in new measures to stop the practice without prejudicing Jazeb's relationships of trust in the business.

Questions

1 Do you have arrangements in your organization to allow reports to be made of wrongdoing where the identity of whistleblowers is protected?

2 How does your organization view whistleblowers? Are they required to make reports of wrongdoing where they see it as a condition of employment, or would they be regarded as undesirables?

3 How confident do you believe employees in your organization are in making reports of wrongdoing, whether or not anonymously?

Jazeb's confidence in the AML compliance team in Case Study 5.6 gave him the courage to make the report without fear of reprisal and the AML compliance team, aware of cultural challenges in the jurisdiction, chose to remove the loophole that allowed misappropriation of funds rather than disciplining the culprit. As well as having an AML compliance contact address, less confident employees may be more likely to report wrongdoing via an anonymous reporting service to minimize their exposure. Continuing to make facilitation payments despite receiving AML training could be attributed to the office manager feeling that he had to satisfy the request for prompt postal delivery or personally suffer the consequences of delays. However, Jazeb's report enabled the company to recognize the gap between accounting practices and local administration. The way the investigation team dealt with the report and implemented local changes to prevent a recurrence gave Ammon a clear rationale as to why the payments could not be made, which provided him with a defence from the pressure of local management, should that occur.

Accountability

Lack of accountability is another key element that can jeopardize the effective application of AML policy, and generally reduce the probability of employees recognizing that there may be an issue at all. Where trust in one's colleagues, the habit of respect for their decisions and lack of accountability meet, AML compliance messages need to be compelling enough to override their combined influence, as illustrated in Case Study 5.7, to effectively reduce organizational risk.

CASE STUDY 5.7: Factors that dampen awareness

Janice and Peter started working together 20 years ago as Personal Assistant and Senior Manager in a high-end estate agency firm, years before AML regulation was introduced and CDD on counterparts was a requirement. Through long association, Peter knew many people in New York and was constantly socializing with them, networking in the industry at launches and events. At one of these events Peter met a counterpart who offered him a stake in his business if he could use his authority to approve a construction deal for him. It was a great opportunity and he was flattered at the offer. Rather than going through the usual on-boarding questionnaire and CDD checks for a new counterpart, Peter agreed to sign off the deal with his own authority without having the due diligence completed. Janice noticed the deal was going through rather quickly and thought it was odd, but she trusted Peter's judgement, knowing that he, and not she, was accountable for client relationships and their due diligence. Anyway, she did not have the counterpart's details and AML compliance was not part of her job description, nor was there a way in the organization for her to report her concern.

In the event, the construction deal was a scam that Peter fell for, and his counterpart 'disappeared'. Peter not only lost his company money, he also lost his job, his career and reputation. After Janice's interview with AML Compliance, when she admired once more the flowers Peter bought for her when she 'looked the other way', she wondered whether, as they were from the proceeds of a scam, the flowers were bought with laundered money?

Questions

1. Does your organization offer AML training to all employees?
2. Do employees in your organization have the responsibility to report activities that are in breach of policies and procedures?
3. Do some employees appear to be overly guided in their activity by their line manager, overriding policies and procedures?
4. Are you confident that, given a clear breach of CDD requirements, all of your employees would blow the whistle and make it known?

Stop and think!

Are your AML internal controls strong enough? Recognizing natural tendencies and local norms as known risks that may minimize or negate the impact of AML policies and procedures can help to strengthen your AML risk control environment. Using Case Studies 5.5, 5.6 and 5.7 as a starting point, make a list of the awareness dampeners in your organization and map out possible resolutions to them. Where do they slot into the activities of the AML strategy wheel (see Chapter 3)?

Fear of reprisals

Fear of reprisals for exposing questionable activities in an organization is a deterrent to employees who notice them. In the case of Michael Woodford as CEO in Case Study 5.4, he had nowhere to hide and his exposure of wrongdoing within Olympus resulted in his departure from the organization and a very difficult period in his life. In less egregious circumstances, it may still not be possible to overcome the fear that whistleblowers experience if senior management do not appear to demonstrate compliance with regulatory requirements themselves, and employees may prefer the anonymity of reporting to a whistleblowing hotline to protect their identity, if the choice is available. Some organizations choose to publish internally the results of investigations, but I prefer to encourage employee confidence by effecting changes within organizational governance that can be seen by employees in amended or new policies and procedures introduced as a positive outcome of their engagement.

Key takeaways

- Introducing a risk-based approach takes time, but it allows tailoring of the AML risk control strategy to make it relevant to your organization, and enables effective provision of more resources to mitigate higher risks.
- Establish country risk as it affects your organization by using internationally recognized measures such as those provided by

Transparency International, considering both the locations of your offices and provision of services.

- People risks are both internal and external, and to de-risk from an AML perspective, no questions should be beyond asking with the purpose of reducing operational risk.
- Knowledge gaps are inevitable, and your AML control environment will benefit from having some flexibility in its design. This does not mean being flexible on the consequences of non-compliance, but having flexibility to amend and adapt policy and procedures without undue delay.
- Assumptions that encourage reduced diligence are all around us. When we encode messages for others such as policies and procedures, they are received by individuals through the filter of their own understanding of the world, which will naturally inform their decisions.

References and further reading

Asia/Pacific Group on Money Laundering (2012) APG Typology Report on Trade Based Money Laundering, available from: www.fatf-gafi.org/media/fatf/documents/reports/Trade_Based_ML_APGReport.pdf (last accessed: 4 February 2018) http://borneobulletin.com.bn/ Fadley Faisal (last accessed 10 April 2017)

Darby, M (1998) In Ponzi We Trust: Borrowing from Peter to pay Paul is a scheme made famous by Charles Ponzi. Who was this crook whose name graces this scam? *Smithsonian Magazine*, December, available from: www.smithsonianmag.com/history/in-ponzi-we-trust-64016168/ (last accessed 4 February 2018)

Faisal, F (2017) Money launderer jailed for first time in Brunei, National, 10/4, available from: http://borneobulletin.com.bn (last accessed 10 April 2017) http://www.fatf-gafi.org/media/fatf/documents/reports/Trade_Based_ML_APGReport.pdf (last accessed 3 May 2017)

Hickey, D (2012) Michael Woodford: Japan's whistle-blower supreme speaks out, Former Olympus exec Michael Woodward shares his thoughts on the company, Japan and more, *Japan Times* 2/12, available from: https://www.japantimes.co.jp/life/2012/12/02/people/japans-whistle-blower-supreme-speaks-out/#.WnbFEq5l_IU (last accessed 4 February 2018)

Transparency International (2017) Corruption Perceptions Index 2016, available from: www.transparency.org/news/feature/corruption_perceptions_index_2016 (last accessed 4 February 2018)

United States Department of Justice (2015) United States v Bernard L Madoff and Related Cases, available from: www.justice.gov/usao-sdny/programs/victim-witness-services/united-states-v-bernard-l-madoff-and-related-cases (last accessed 4 February 2018)

Woodford, M (2012) *Exposure: From President to whistleblower at Olympus*, Penguin Books, London

Product and delivery channel risk

06

Product and delivery channel risk is all about what activities your organization is involved in and how it reaches its customers. Does anyone from your organization actually meet your customers in person, or are your customers remote? Are you dealing in high-value goods or accepting cash transactions? When assessing the risk of your product, service or delivery channel consider whether they can readily fulfil the primary objective of money launderers: to disguise the source of the property or funds being laundered. Does your organization offer a useful vehicle by not fully identifying the source of funds? Can your products or services be used to conceal the beneficial ownership of the property or funds? Could money launderers be using your organization to provide an extra layer of distance between their crime and its proceeds? Whether your products and services exist in the physical or virtual world, you can be assured that criminals have assessed them as to their use and how risky they would be as a conduit for the proceeds of their crimes.

So, what makes a product or delivery channel attractive to money launderers? How do we monitor our transactions? Do we rely on technology too heavily or not enough? The answers to these questions help AML professionals to more readily recognize the risks their organization needs to address. In this chapter we will consider:

- Product risk.
- Delivery channel risk.
- Transaction monitoring.
- Reliance upon technology.
- Keeping auditable records.

Product risk

There are products that are naturally low risk, being of less interest to money launderers, and others that are at the higher end of the risk spectrum, but how do you know which is which? Essentially, low-risk products are those that require investment over a long period and/or have restrictions on how much money can be put in or taken out of them and when. They include life insurance products for which there is a low premium, contributory pension schemes and highly regulated, limited investment savings plans. Higher-risk products include those taken out with a lump sum of money that can be cancelled within a cooling off period or soon after, perhaps with a penalty the criminal does not care about as he or she just wants another layer in the money laundering process that is provided by using your organization's product. Consider the products below with their indicators of risk.

Lower-risk product indicators

1. *Insurance products*, including general insurance, car, house and contents; regular premium life assurance and annuities.
2. *Pension products:* where payments are made over a number of years and there are restrictions on withdrawals or redemption.
3. *Investment savings products:* where there is a limit on the amount of funds that can be invested.

Higher-risk product indicators

1. *High-risk products, including insurance*, are those that accept cash payments, high-value single payments or payments from third parties; can be liquidated quickly and/or without significant cost, or can be traded on a secondary market or used as security for a loan.
2. *Wealth management products* provide the money launderer with reputable fund management, including: investment and banking with very high-value transactions, services that allow transfers across many jurisdictions, a culture of attentiveness and confidentiality by banking employees to discreetly manage their client

portfolios, services in jurisdictions with bank secrecy legislation, services using sophisticated non-standard products that may include offshore or shell companies, personal investment vehicles or trusts.

3 *Wholesale investments and securities trading*, where securities are any tradable financial asset. They are highly liquid: quickly tradable, available around the globe, so the money launderer can follow the sun to get access to an open market anytime; deal with large volumes of high-value international transactions making dirty money hard to spot; trading with non-standard and sophisticated products.

4 *Single premium* bonds, investments, insurance: financial services products that can be purchased with a high-value premium, especially where they come with a cooling-off period during which the purchaser can withdraw the entire amount invested without incurring costs. These products remain high risk after the cooling-off period even where penalty charges are incurred for early redemption as, for the money launderer, the funds remain within the layering process, biding their time before putting the funds to use.

5 *Real estate*, especially at the high end and when they are: paid for in cash rather than with a mortgage; purchased by a foreign buyer from a country in the lower half of the Transparency International Corruption Perceptions Index; purchased by a services company for a client, where due diligence is carried out on the services company and not on the actual client.

6 *Company service providers, lawyers and accountants*, the gatekeepers who: hold client accounts on behalf of their customers; have professional privilege of information and expertise in its management to benefit clients, maintaining confidentiality; act on behalf of clients in setting up company structures and movement of funds to maximize the benefit of value to clients.

7 *Online gambling* is legal in some countries but not in others. The elements that make online gambling a high risk include: the use of stolen credit cards to pay for stake money; the software for online gambling is often held offshore, so outside of the regulatory

reach of the gambler's jurisdiction, which makes it very difficult to gain access to the records of the gambling transaction; online gambling sites hide the gambler, and so hide the criminals who use them. As virtual gambling sites use virtual payment systems, this is rich ground in which criminals and money launderers can operate without detection.

8. *Dealers in high-value goods* are businesses or sole traders that, under 4MLD make or accept cash payments of €10,000 or more in exchange for goods, where cash payments include currency and transfers to bank accounts. High-value payments may be made in one amount of €10,000 or more, or by several payments adding up to or above the threshold amount for the goods, either business-facing as a wholesale transaction or customer-facing as a retail transaction. Single high-value cash payments for large quantities of lower-value goods are also included. Dealers in high-value goods do not need to own the goods they sell, the test is whether they give or receive high-value cash payments for them. Examples include antique and fine art dealers, yacht brokers, car dealers, builders and jewellers.
9. *Cash-rich businesses*, as criminal money is co-mingled with legitimate funds and introduced to the banking system. Popular businesses in this category include: restaurants, bistros and cafés; launderettes and dry cleaning services, and florists.
10. *Non face-to-face financial services*. These proliferated with the advent of the internet and are very useful to money launderers because as long as verification of identity is fulfilled, an account can be opened. False identification and verification documents can be purchased from criminals in a non face-to-face transaction online. The money launderer can operate from the comfort of his or her computer terminal with minimum cost and maximum anonymity.

In some organizations, it has been the virtue of product development gurus to come up with financial products with activities outside of the jurisdictional regulatory framework, to outsmart the regulators and ensure their product can make gains unimpeded. This is why some regulators are moving towards an outcomes-based regulatory framework.

> **Note: Regulatory compliance frameworks**
>
> Rules-based frameworks set out precise rules and products can be designed to be just outside them. Principles-based regimes require industry players to adhere to guiding principles. This does not work if the guiding minds of obliged entities do not have any principles. Outcomes-based regulatory requirements give companies the freedom to design the products as they see fit, but if the regulator does not like the outcomes, disciplinary action will follow.

Risks specific to providing products and services to wealthy clients

The United Kingdom's Joint Money Laundering Steering Group sets out specific risks of providing products and services to wealthy and powerful clients:

- Wealthy and powerful clients may be reluctant or unwilling to provide adequate documents, details and explanations when applying for the products and services of your organization. The situation is exacerbated where the client enjoys a high public profile, and where he or she wields political economic power or influence, as discussed in Chapter 5.
- Multiple and complex accounts – clients often have many accounts in more than one jurisdiction, either within the same firm or group, or with different firms. Do you check the beneficial ownership of products used by clients in your organization sufficiently to identify obfuscation of ownership by the use of different vehicles?
- Cultures of confidentiality – wealth management clients often seek reassurance that their business will be conducted discreetly. See Case Study 1.2 for the effects on Coutts & Co. bank in the UK of conducting weak Client Due Diligence (CDD) and then providing financial services products when they came to regulatory attention.
- Concealment – the misuse of services such as offshore trusts and the availability of structures such as shell companies help to maintain an element of secrecy about beneficial ownership of funds.

Does your organization provide company services, such as the establishment and maintenance of offshore trusts and shell companies for clients? These are high-risk products, of use to high-risk clients. Protect your organization by applying enhanced AML compliance attention to these services and the clients that use them.

- Countries with statutory banking secrecy – there is a culture of secrecy in certain jurisdictions, supported by local legislation, in which wealth management is available.
- Movement of funds – the transmission of funds and other assets by private clients often involves high-value transactions, requiring rapid transfers to be made across accounts in different countries and regions of the world. When providing services that allow these transmissions to take place, ensure that your systems and controls include detailed identifiers to assist tracking precisely where the funds are going.
- The use of concentration accounts, ie multi-client pooled/omnibus type accounts used to collect together funds from a variety of sources for onward transmission, is seen as a potential major risk.
- Credit – the extension of credit to clients who use their assets as collateral also poses a money laundering risk unless the lender is satisfied that the origin and source of the underlying asset is legitimate. Establishing whether the client is the legitimate owner of the asset comes at the start of AML activity when he or she is applying for credit using it as collateral. Providing credit on the security of high-value stolen goods will not improve the reputation of your organization should it come to the attention of local regulators!
- Commercial activity conducted through a personal account so as to deceive the banker. This activity can be identified when offering banking services by asking the client during initial CDD what purpose the account is to serve, in which jurisdictions the client expects it to operate and what sort of transactions are expected to go through it. The client may not give a clear picture, of course, if the intention is to deceive, but it gives a good starting point for monitoring the account to see if the client's stated intentions match up to reality. If not, up goes the red flag for AML investigations!

Note

Always remember that the wealthier clients are, the more confident they are likely to be. They will know how much the organization managing their wealth is likely to profit by providing them with products and services. These are important clients, and keeping them is a business imperative. Unsurprising then, that wealth management houses may be disinclined to ask their wealthy clients unwelcome probing questions that may prompt them to go elsewhere. This could have an impact on employee bonuses and company profit. Once criminals have sufficient proceeds of crime to qualify for wealth management services, they can mingle with legitimate wealthy clients and use the culture of hesitancy to avoid divulging details while expecting the benefit of the products and services of AML-regulated entities. Their unwillingness to provide such information fits well with the stance of other wealthy and powerful clients and, by allowing the criminal to get away with it, those banks and financial services organizations are playing right into their hands.

Delivery channel risk

The new internet-enabled payment methods have given rise to a host of new ways to commit fraud and money laundering transactions online. Transaction laundering comes in several forms. For example, in payment services, an issuing bank has an arrangement with an acquirer to accept card payments made by customers for goods and services provided by merchants. The banks and acquirers are subject to the AML legislation of their jurisdiction, as are their Independent Sales Organizations (ISOs) with the payment terminals, leaving the merchants as the recognized weakest link in the process – retail outlets, to you and me. Types of transaction laundering include the following.

Front company

Transaction laundering takes place by a criminal using a front company when the company itself, say a café, serves tea and cakes as its legitimate business, but also launders money from the drugs it sells to customers at the same time. The drugs are paid for with the tea and cakes, and the Merchant Category Code for transmitting the payment from card to acquirer is standard for the business. False transactions are processed to launder money made from the drug dealing, not from selling tea and cakes.

Pass-through company

A business such as the fitness studio in Case Study 6.1 agrees or is forced to allow the use of its legitimate payment services account to launder money by a criminal party in a number of ways:

- It can allow a payment link to be embedded on an illegal entity's website that makes the payments through the legitimate company's processes.
- It can actively enter the illegal entity's sales manually into the payment system. This is very difficult to detect when carrying out monitoring.
- It can engage in an arrangement with the illegal entity or criminal whereby a commission is paid for the use of payment services.

Funnel account

A business, set up legitimately with a merchant services agreement, then accepts credit card charges from companies that do not have merchant processing accounts of their own, in contravention of their agreement. See Case Study 6.2 for Lancore Services' attempt to have Barclaycard Business pay them monies that had been paid through their merchant terminals, from illegal activity.

It is the responsibility of the banks, acquirers and ISOs to keep merchants that abuse their payment processing accounts out of the payments system, but their detection can be very difficult and their methods of abusing the system vary. Consider Case Study 6.1, where the proprietor of a fitness studio found her trust being abused by a new but attractive and well-known baseball celebrity, who convinced her to process card payments to her own detriment.

CASE STUDY 6.1: Abuse of card terminals

An established fitness studio owner in Scottsdale, AZ, accepted payments for services using her merchant terminal. Her business was successful, and when she applied for merchant services she passed CDD checks with her provider and had been using the service for her legitimate business for some time. In 2015, she met Chris Gatling, an ex US National Basketball Association player on a dating website and they talked about his internet businesses that created websites and fixed credit. What she did not know was that she was being groomed by him and her real attraction to him was the access she could give him to financial services.

He convinced her about his businesses sufficiently for her to agree to charge credit cards for him through her merchant terminal, and the 10 per cent of the dollar amounts he offered her in commission would certainly help financially, even though she had to accept giving him his 90 per cent share in cash before they were payable by the credit card providers. However, some of the payments were being refused. The card holders alerted the credit card companies when they saw the charges on their statements. When police investigated it was found that Gatling was involved in several illegal online businesses, with the purpose of gathering credit card numbers that were used in payment for services not authorized by the legitimate credit card holders. These charges were payable by the fitness studio owner as it was she who enabled the fraud by allowing Gatling access to her merchant terminal. It was she who became the victim of Gatling's crime as she was liable for the services that were authorized by its use, which amounted to US$90,000. This was a disaster for the fitness studio owner as she not only lost her business, she then lost the ability to earn an income from it. Although Gatling's operation was run from a single call centre in Phoenix, AZ, alleged victims came forward from all around the United States.

Questions

1. If you have card machines that take electronic payments, do you know whether any other affiliate entity or individual outside of your organization is given access to deposit payments into them, either electronically or in cash raised from their own activities?
2. Is any individual or entity outside of your organization able to make or receive payments through the access you have to financial services?
3. Are your AML controls sufficiently robust to prevent your organization being used by third parties, or are they susceptible to fraud or money laundering card transactions?

In addition to adding cash deposits to the takings of a card terminal, it is possible for transaction launderers to funnel payments made in criminal activity from websites other than the merchant's own by using their card terminal to clean the money. In allowing this, merchants would be disregarding their agreement with their acquirer, flouting AML laws and, like the fitness studio owner in Case Study 6.1, they stand to lose both money and potentially their business. Financial services regulation requires participants to keep criminal activity out of their processes and practices, regardless of whether the transaction is carried out face-to-face, over the phone or online, and even though this type of fraud and money laundering is fairly new, the regulations that cover it are well established.

Stop and think

Where are the transaction vulnerabilities in your organization?

CASE STUDY 6.2: Lancore Services Ltd v Barclays Bank plc

In November 2005, Lancore Services Ltd, positioning itself as a kitchenware mail order and telephone sales company, was granted a merchant service facility by Barclaycard Business to process credit and debit card payments. However, after less than three months of operation, Barclaycard Business suspended its merchant facility. Instead of an expected transaction flow declared before signing the agreement, a much higher monetary flow was passing through the payment service, which raised red flags in the Barclays' system. Rather than processing payments for kitchenware, Lancore was allowing the use of its payment service by third parties, which was not permitted in its merchant services agreement.

After review by the Special Investigations Section at Barclaycard Business, it was found that Lancore was engaged in unauthorized third-party transactions by processing payments for the sale of high-risk and sometimes illegal pharmaceutical products and pornographic material. At that time Barclaycard Business was holding around £1.4 million in different currencies ready for payment to Lancore, and it decided not to make the onward payment. Lancore made a claim for the retained money and then an appeal for Barclaycard Business to pay it, but Lancore had clearly broken their agreement and

Barclaycard Business had the right to retain the money. The judge, Lord Justice Rimer, rejected Lancore's claim for payment. The kitchenware company was essentially a front for processing illegal payments.

Questions

If your organization is a user of card payment services:

1. What internal controls do you have to ensure that merchant terminals are only used for legitimate transactions within the merchant services agreement?
2. What sort of due diligence does your acquirer carry out on your use of the card terminal?
3. How do you ensure that your organization remains in compliance with your merchant/acquirer agreement?

Transaction monitoring

After the attacks on the New York World Trade Center on 9 September 2001, the Financial Action Task Force (FATF) introduced its Special Recommendations (SRs), as discussed in Chapter 1. Of these, SR VII required the licensing of money transmitters, who must gather information to enable identification of the person requesting the transfer including name, address and the account number from which the funds are to be drawn for the transfer. Transfers requested without that information raise a red flag, and are deemed suspicious activity.

On revision of the FATF Recommendations in 2012, SR VII became Recommendation 16 (R16), which has essentially the same requirements of identification of the originator and the beneficiary, which must remain with the transaction from beginning to end for tracking purposes. (See Table 1.1 for FATF Recommendations as revised in 2012.) The financial institution used for the wire transfer is required by R16 to monitor them, and have checks on the monitoring system to identify transfers with incomplete originator and beneficiary information. Having monitored the transfers, these institutions need to have the ability to stop the transaction by freezing the funds en route to their beneficiary, and ensure that neither party is on a relevant trade sanctions list.

> **Note: FATF Recommendations**
>
> R16. Countries should ensure that financial institutions monitor wire transfers for the purpose of detecting those which lack required originator and/or beneficiary information and take appropriate measures...
> Revised 2012

Transaction monitoring systems, introduced to facilitate this, gather information from the start to finish of a wire transfer, and provide all of the information required to produce auditable records if appropriate trigger points are put in place by the organization. There is more on reliance on technology below, but first let us consider the elements that make up effective risk-based transaction monitoring.

1 Choose a vendor

Consider the following points when choosing a transaction monitoring system from a vendor:

- Does the vendor have an established client base including organizations in a similar market to your own? Seek feedback from them to establish whether the vendor has the resources to deliver the service, provide ongoing support and regular system upgrades.
- The system needs to be sophisticated enough to filter transaction data to the specific needs of your organization, and flexible enough to deal with data from legacy systems where relevant. If this is not possible, widen your vendor search or mitigate the risk by implementing procedures to deal with the data.
- Liaise with your system provider to establish detailed system configuration and maintain an ongoing relationship to ensure it is aware early of relevant organizational changes that may impact your requirements of the system.
- Review the case management capability of the system. Can it track activity at all stages of the monitoring process? It will need to track all enquiry points with records of resolution to enable active management to minimize this risk to your organization.

2 Define specific risks

Identifying broad risks will give you a starting point for your transaction monitoring programme, but it is the specific risks identified that give you the granularity to apply triggers in automated systems that capture data, filter it and raise red flags.

3 Red flags

Transaction monitoring systems provide for the organization to put in place rules-based alerts where a transaction, for example:

- does not have all of the identification details of the originator or beneficiary;
- is above a certain level, either set by regulation or identified as relevant in the risk analysis;
- is requesting transfer of funds to a jurisdiction that does not align with customer profiling established via the CDD process;
- does not fit with the customer profile identified in the CDD process.

4 Train employees

Your transaction monitoring system provider should be able to provide employee training that covers how the system operates and how to optimize its performance. Employees then need training on what to do when using the system to ensure your AML regulatory requirements are covered. This is where your policies and processes come in. If well written they will provide a guidebook on what to do when red flags are raised, and be a go-to resource for employees wanting to know what to do next.

5 Escalation to management

Management information from transaction monitoring provides the opportunity to give the right information straight from the system to the right people at timely intervals for them to have appropriate oversight and meet reporting requirements.

6 Management information

Design management information output from transaction monitoring from the outset, before selecting a vendor, if you are using one. You need to evidence activity for regulatory requirements and provide readily accessible information for AML compliance review in as near to real time as possible. Get input from those involved in the on-boarding process and monitoring, and from those providing the reports to regulators and the board. This will create awareness and engagement, and allow you to be better prepared with all of their ideas and requirements when you frame the expectations of a transaction monitoring system suitable for the needs of your organization.

7 Quality assurance

The quality of information gathered will depend on the rules written into the system to produce red flags. If these are inaccurate or insufficient, the data gathered will not be useful on a rubbish in–rubbish out basis. Regular risk-based sample monitoring is essential to provide quality assurance and improve controls.

8 Maintenance of the system

Whichever transaction monitoring system you use, it will need active management and maintenance to ensure that it is producing the output you expect. Needs change over time, so consider the system flexibility you may require to incorporate the effects of new risks emerging, including the rapid pace of technological advancement that may increase the number of unknown unknowns.

Note: Red flags

A 'red flag' is a warning flag that there may be a problem, a sign of alert. This term is widely used, and here it is a warning that there may be issues with a transaction that need to be investigated further. Potentially temporary application of the brakes is required to prevent a money laundering transaction from passing through your organization.

Reliance upon technology

The apparent reliability of modern technology together with great sales pitches of vendor firms may provide a high level of confidence in the service provided to fulfil a regulatory requirement or business need. A drawback with this is that it takes people to input the red flag indicators, and people make errors. Even if they do not, risks change and the red flag indicators will need to change with them, and older technology that depends upon algorithms and thresholds may struggle to keep pace with the evolution of money laundering techniques in the online era.

However, even older technology solutions have their uses. As an example of thresholds working well when inputted to a transaction monitoring system, let's think of a criminal wishing to place large sums of cash into the financial services system by using bank accounts. All a regulator has to do to affect the activity is to change a reporting threshold and the criminal has to give those people he uses to make deposits into the bank accounts, known as 'smurfs', instructions to pay in smaller amounts of money to keep under the bank's checking threshold. This is likely to cost the criminal more and depositing the whole amount will take longer. In this example, the criminal is using smurfs to ensure that the red flag indicators set in the bank's technology are not activated. This means more work for the smurfs as they take smaller amounts to deposit into, probably, a greater number of banks to avoid detection and hide the criminal money safely in the financial system.

Note

In money laundering terms, a 'smurf' is a criminal at the bottom of the pay scale whose job it is to divide up larger amounts of cash from criminal activity and make deposits into multiple bank accounts small enough to escape detection. The amount of deposit is set below the regulatory threshold for mandatory checking so that large amounts can be gradually introduced to the financial system. This is the placement stage of money laundering, as discussed in Chapter 1.

New technology using advanced analytics is more intelligent and therefore more adaptable to changing requirements, but it is also very complex, requiring more advanced skills in understanding its capabilities. It will still be the AML Responsible Officer who has to explain how it helps to prevent the organization being used as a vehicle for money launderers, of course, so this is likely to represent a steep learning curve! New technology is further accelerating the speed with which financial transactions take place, be it via a computer terminal, mobile phone, tablet… the list goes on, further increasing the complexity of monitoring programmes.

Stop and think

Is anyone in the AML compliance or fraud departments of your organization sufficiently knowledgeable to confidently walk the auditors through your transaction monitoring systems?

Keeping auditable records

Think 'auditable records' from the very start of AML process mapping in your organization. Keeping auditable records of your AML control activity is not only a regulatory requirement, it is a really useful way of tracking progress and issues as they occur. I have found that the automation of processes in online workflows provides full auditable records of processes, even when they are not fully automated. Consider the efforts of Clara in Case Study 6.3 when moving her organization from operating fully manual to semi-automated pre-approvals for employee spending on gifts and entertainment. Delivering this service internally to employees has enabled Clara to provide appropriate records to her auditors at minimal notice.

Stop and think

The services you provide to your organization matter too! Thinking about the products and services that AML compliance provides to the organization may help to focus on their effectiveness rather than the cost or time spent on their development.

CASE STUDY 6.3: Acquiring auditable records by moving online

Clara's global role included ensuring that anti-bribery and corruption controls were in place, sufficient to withstand audit in compliance with the Sarbanes-Oxley Act. Although the requirement to adhere to policy had been in place for many years, Clara noticed that there were insufficient requests to approve the giving of gifts and entertainment coming through for her attention. Starting with the Middle Eastern offices, Clara provided mandatory face-to-face training for all employees in the Foreign Corrupt Practices Act and the UK Bribery Act, both having extraterritorial powers. She identified responsible individuals in Sales, Marketing and Finance to control gifts and entertainment requests locally and, in a painful process that took two to three years, all of the relevant employees and their management became aware of what they must do. They just did not want to follow the process. Finance wasn't particularly interested as the policy belonged to AML Compliance, even though payments for the gifts and entertainment have to be approved as a financial control.

Finally Clara found a solution. She called a meeting with the heads of Marketing and Finance and told them that as at least on one whole continent their employees were still ignoring her, she would withdraw from the process herself, and hand it back to them, the budget holder and the payment maker. Immediately she had their attention, and in that very meeting it was decided to build an online workflow for the approvals. Clara also received support from Sales, and mandatory online training was written, produced and given to all relevant employees. Within three months, gifts and entertainment approvals moved online, with review and sign-off from all relevant stakeholders, Marketing and Finance included. The data gathered was used as management information for senior regional leaders and all responsibilities for the management of the anti-bribery and corruption risk were in the hands of the right people, and ready for audit. Gone was the opportunity for internal fraud and money laundering via that process. Clara handed it over to an AML compliance team member for management, and soon found another gap that she needed to fill in her efforts to minimize the risk of employees in her own organization taking advantage of process weaknesses. The auditable records would be available from the first entry of the pre-approval process, as everything was submitted and accepted via a very simple but effective online process.

Questions

1. How do you gather auditable records from your internal processes?
2. Are your auditable processes online, or are they carried out by e-mail and individual agreement by the parties concerned?
3. Do you have an intranet, or could you access the intranet of your organization?
4. What support would you need to move your internal approval processes – services – online?

In the case of Clara in Case Study 6.3, the auditable records requirement changed from being almost impossible to manage using e-mails and signed documents being kept and monitored in the business areas, to an online system already available to employees once access was gained to it, that satisfied the requirement for auditable records by actually minimizing the input needed. Whatever the size of your organization, seek out the systems purchased already and find a way to use them to minimize your workload and enhance your AML compliance programme. This is the work of investigation and opportunity: use it.

Key takeaways

- Product risk. There are identifiers of product risk that ring true across the products of obliged entities, as detailed earlier in this chapter. When considering the veracity of claims made by interested parties in your organization or wishing to do business with your organization, keep true to the basics and use these identifiers as the ground rules upon which to establish AML risks.
- Delivery channel risk. Since the advent of the internet, delivery channel risk has become more and more important in AML risk assessment, not least because of the irrelevance of national boundaries, which used to apply a natural braking system to the transaction process. Now online payments facilitate transactions very effectively, national boundaries are irrelevant and there are literally millions of transactions in the capital markets and investments arena that take place every day.

- As a result of increased speed and the near anonymity allowed by non face-to-face transaction services, transaction monitoring is a major part of AML assurance in banks and investment services.
- Reliance on technology remains a risk as where it becomes out of date or the correct checking parameters are omitted, the rubbish in–rubbish out tenet applies. In my observation, there is a tendency to have criteria agreed by senior leaders that go out of date quickly, requiring considerable effort to renew, during which time the technology is becoming ever more out of date. Temper your reliance on technology with acceptance of the change process in your organization. Your time spent influencing it to be more efficient will probably be time very well spent.
- Gathering and keeping records sufficient for audit can consume inordinate quantities of time and resources, or virtually none at all. Seek to benefit from the advantages of modern technology and gather auditable information from the first keystroke. Make redundant paper files kept in satellite offices (yes, they do still exist!) and implement processes where auditable records are produced online and can be viewed from wherever in the world the AML compliance function resides. Everyone involved in the process will benefit from the time saved, and AML compliance will have systems-based records to produce for audit.

References and further reading

Directive (EU) 2015/849 of the European Parliament and of The Council of 20 May 2015 on the prevention of the use of the financial system for the purposes of money laundering or terrorist financing, amending Regulation (EU) No 648/2012 of the European Parliament and of the Council, and repealing Directive 2005/60/EC of the European Parliament and of the Council and Commission Directive 2006/70/EC (Fourth Money Laundering Directive)

The Joint Money Laundering Steering Group Guidance (2012) Prevention of money laundering/combating terrorist financing Part II Sectoral Guidance 5, Wealth Management. London, available from: file:///C:/Users/Rosemary/Downloads/BBA01-389166-v2-Part_II_Board_approved_Dec_2011_CLEAN.pdf (last accessed 7 February 2018)

Lancore Services Limited v Barclays Bank plc [2009] EWCA Civ 752 Case No: 6MA30009, available from: http://www.bailii.org/ew/cases/EWCA/Civ/2009/752.html (last accessed 6 February 2018)

MONEYVAL (2008) Typology Research: Use of securities in money laundering schemes, available from: www.coe.int/t/dghl/ monitoring/moneyval/typologies/MONEYVAL(2008)24Reptyp_securities.pdf (last accessed 6 February 2018)

MONEYVAL (2012) Research Report: Criminal money flows on the Internet: methods, trends and multi-stakeholder counteraction, available from: https://rm.coe.int/research-report-criminal-money-flows-on-the-internet-methods-trends-an/168071509a (last accessed 6 February 2018)

Platt, S (2015) *Criminal Capital: How the finance industry facilitates crime*, Palgrave Macmillan, London

USA Today (2015) Ex-NBA All-Star Chris Gatling arrested in online credit card scam 30/5, available from: www.usatoday.com/story/sports/nba/2015/05/30/chris-gatling-arrested--online-credit-card-scam/28218695/ (last accessed 6 February 2018)

van der Does de Willebois, E, Halter, E M, Harrison, R A, Park, Ji Won, Sharman, J C (2011) *The Puppet Masters, How the corrupt use legal structures to hide stolen assets and what to do about it. Stolen asset recovery initiative*, The World Bank, available from: https://star.worldbank.org/star/sites/star/files/puppetmastersv1.pdf (last accessed 23 January 2018)

Regulators 07

External reporting and Financial Intelligence Unit activity

In this chapter we will look into aspects of regulatory activity, external reporting and the activities of Financial Intelligence Units.

This chapter covers:

- Increasing effectiveness of Financial Intelligence Units collaboration.
- Recognizing and reporting suspicious activity.
- Regulatory consequences of failures in anti-money laundering controls.

The big picture: increasing effectiveness of FIU collaboration

As discussed in Chapter 1, FIUs are national agencies responsible for receiving, analysing and transmitting disclosures on suspicious transactions to the competent authorities of their jurisdictions (International Monetary Fund, 2004). They were first established by the original members of the Financial Action Task Force (FATF) in the 1980s to be local hubs of AML activity. At that time there was no body of information for FIUs to draw on as guidance when countries engaged in drafting AML legislation to provide controls. As their AML knowledge and skills grew, the FIUs' information bank and trust of each other grew also. They began more readily to recognize suspicious activity as having certain characteristics and worked with FATF to publish typologies to alert others to trends in criminal activity, enabling FIUs to become significant agents for change in the fight against money laundering.

Before internet connectivity and when financial institutions were more single country-based there was little cooperation between FIUs apart from in cases of drug trafficking. However, with developments in communications and payments via the internet, FIUs began to work more closely together to follow the money. To enable this, the establishment of good cross-border communications to create understanding and trust is essential for FIUs, to ensure that they do not compete in the investigation of cases or waste time duplicating work, so complementing each other's activities and maximizing their resources. When FIUs overcome national protectionism, they are more able to combat attempts by criminals to launder money across their borders, and work together to embed consistent implementation of soft law conventions in local laws and regulations. Technological developments have transformed the way that financial services in securities and banking operate in terms of both speed and accessibility, providing organizations with greater opportunities to reach potential customers and greater challenges in identifying a clear, effective, cross-border regulatory environment in which to do so.

This is seen in organizations that choose to grow by having their head office in one jurisdiction and creating or acquiring subsidiaries in others to give a 'family tree' of entities across the globe. The transfer of intellectual capital from the head office to subsidiaries in other countries helps to build their international capability and brings them into the realm of international conventions that transcend the local political and economic power base. As these global corporations buy up local entities and change their names to that of the parent company, local perceptions of it and its power relations become more international, even if the employees remain the same. The clear boundaries of sovereignty become blurred and the simple way to implement coherent financial services regulatory controls is to adopt international soft law conventions that broadly cover local requirements, allowing for local amendment. Indeed, this tendency has been claimed as an explanation of why countries tend to adhere to international soft law: 'The modern transformation of sovereignty has remade international law, so that international law norms now help construct national identities and interests through a process of justificatory discourse' (Koh, 1997).

Where a global organization makes a local acquisition and attempts to embed norms of international law, it may meet a previously more isolated culture in the board and employees. This in turn may affect the ability of the acquired company to embrace good corporate governance, depending on the extent to which democracy, accountability, fairness and transparency are already embedded in the local culture (more on this in Chapter 8). No matter what state of governance already exists, the acquisition will need to review the operational controls required by FATF, and perhaps begin to work with the local FIU in making Suspicious Activity Reports (SAR) for the first time. In this way, global corporations further the AML agenda and assist the engagement of local FIUs with their own interaction across borders in a virtuous spiral. It represents more opportunities for AML professionals to reduce the risks of the global entity by implementing AML controls that reduce risks in the subsidiary.

By their very nature, money launderers like to move money, and themselves, across borders to jurisdictions that may have more robust AML regulations but also offer greater safety in which to enjoy the fruits of their money laundering labour. As discussed in Chapter 5, AML regulatory regimes tend to harmonize activity with international expectations, and an example of consecutive activity by FIUs was highlighted in Case Study 2.2, when, in 2012, China stepped up its compliance in response to Garth Peterson being convicted in the United States for paying bribes to Chinese government officials. In this instance, communication between the two jurisdictions was seen to be at an early, immature stage, with the US Department of Justice passing over the file to the Chinese authorities only after it had completed its investigation and its case was developed. With the information received from the US government, the Chinese were willing and able to take decisive action against the government official receiving the bribes.

That was in 2012. With the passage of time and growing confidence gained from early exchanges of information, greater willingness to collaborate can be seen between FIUs. There is evidence of a trend in financial crime, including money laundering, being carried out by the same organization across multiple jurisdictions. The FIUs collaborate on investigations with sufficient trust between them to allow a lead FIU to emerge for each particular case by agreement, and for the others to use that information, rather than following their own separate paths. Speaking at a conference in London in April 2017, Matthew Wagstaff, Joint Head of Bribery and Corruption at the UK's Serious Fraud Office, described how in the 2017 Rolls Royce case, the FIUs in the United States, Brazil and Britain collaborated on the investigation, demonstrating a move towards better multi-agency cooperation on bribery cases. The new approach has the effect of tying together the investigations of all cooperating jurisdictions, avoiding duplication of effort and maximizing the effectiveness of FIU resources. This in turn allows the investigation of a greater number of cases worldwide with improved efficiencies, and there is plenty of evidence that FIUs are more effectively working together to fight corruption and money laundering. Consider Case Study 3.1 on Siemens, and Case Study 4.1, where multiple FIUs worked together to stop the Telia organization paying bribes to government officials in Uzbekistan and to hold it to account for its criminal activities.

Working as AML professionals now, the AML regulatory foundations are firmly in place, but criminals continue to devise new ways of defrauding companies and individuals alike, so recognizing suspicious activity and reporting it to your local FIU is an essential part of assisting law enforcement to catch money launderers and protect your company from inadvertently assisting a criminal act. Far from being a de-risked and pedestrian activity, AML is likely to be investigative and with ground-breaking innovations. A recent trend in fraud is invoice diversion, where the criminal hacks into the e-mail network of an organization and money mules attempt to divert invoice payments to their own account for a commission, as in Case Study 7.2. This constantly moving risk environment, I believe, makes financial crime, including AML, a very interesting area in which to develop one's career, especially with the international opportunities that have opened up with technological advances and globalization.

Recognizing and reporting suspicious activity

In AML, recognizing suspicious activity is inherently subjective because there is a judgement to be made. Personal judgement is itself subjective, and there does not have to be proof for a person to have suspicion of wrongdoing. Attempts have been made to define 'suspicion' in law, and in the case of Hussein v Chong Fook Kam, Lord

Devlin defined suspicion as follows: 'Suspicion in its ordinary meaning is a state of conjecture or surmise where proof is lacking: I suspect but I cannot prove.' Another attempt at defining suspicion in the UK courts, R v Da Silva, was quoted in the case of Shah v HSBC:

> The defendant must think that there is a possibility, which is more than fanciful, that the relevant facts exist. A vague feeling of unease would not suffice. But (the UK Proceeds of Crime Act 2002) does not require suspicion to be 'clear' or 'firmly grounded' and targeted on 'specific facts' or based on 'reasonable grounds'.

Note

After reporting a suspicious transaction request to an FIU, the reporting entity must await consent from it to continue. The reporting entity is forbidden to inform the person who made the suspicious transaction request of the reason for the delay, as that would be 'tipping off'.

As recognizing suspicious activity is a cornerstone of AML controls, it makes a good starting point for newly obliged entities to focus on. Helpfully, when suspicious activity is detected and an SAR is sent to the local FIU, the obliged entity is bound by legal obligations that were tested in the case of Shah v HSBC Private Bank (see Case Study 7.1). Mr and Mrs Shah were aware of the contractual obligations of the bank and made a case for repayment of losses when HSBC delayed carrying out an instruction, but this was not allowed as the requirement of the UK Proceeds of Crime Act 2002 (POCA) 'trumped' the contractual obligations that HSBC had with the Shahs.

CASE STUDY 7.1: Shah v HSBC

Mr and Mrs Shah, based in Zimbabwe, brought a case against HSBC because the bank had failed to comply with their instructions to make a payment, which resulted in losses to Mr and Mrs Shah in the region of US$300 million. HSBC did not provide Mr and Mrs Shah with a reason for the delay in making the payment, apart from that it was in compliance with their statutory obligations. These 'statutory obligations' were Sections 327 to 329 of POCA. HSBC could not let the Shahs know they had made an SAR because, having made the SAR to SOCA, giving any details would amount to tipping them off, which is prohibited under Section 333A of POCA. HSBC eventually received consent from SOCA to make the payment, but by that time the Zimbabwean authorities, thinking the Shahs were being investigated for money laundering offences, had frozen their assets in Zimbabwe.

Having suffered both huge embarrassment and financial loss, Mr Shah quite reasonably asked HSBC why it had delayed in making the payment, but in compliance with tipping-off provisions HSBC declined to comment. Court action and appeals followed, the outcomes of which have very helpfully provided clarification to organizations on the application in law of their AML control environment in the UK.

The Shahs' challenge did not succeed at appeal, the AML nominated officer at HSBC having, 'honestly and genuinely suspected that the funds were criminal property when he submitted his report to SOCA'. It all started when a member of staff had a suspicion, and Mr Shah's explanation for the movements of funds was not sufficient to satisfy concerns. The case was considered internally at HSBC and it submitted an SAR to SOCA, which HSBC later accepted in court, 'was lacking and its wording was very poor'. This will not have assisted SOCA in coming to a speedy decision on whether or not to provide consent to proceed with the transaction.

It may be that Mr Shah, clearly a very wealthy and probably influential person, was not used to having to explain his actions and preferred not to give details of his financial affairs to a bank employee. This is not unusual with high net worth clients, as discussed in Chapter 6. This hesitance to provide a clear account would tend to increase rather than reduce the suspicion in the bank employee that the funds were, in fact, the proceeds of crime, especially as Zimbabwe was a high-risk jurisdiction and the source of funds was unknown.

Although the results of HSBC's compliance with POCA in this case unfortunately resulted in detriment to the Shahs, the case and appeals have provided valuable insight into how the provisions of POCA will be applied in practice in English Law. Fortunately, the FIU process has become more streamlined and the timeline for the initial review process can be shorter, which should help to prevent others suffering detriment where SARs are made and transactions are legitimate. As a result of the Shah case, AML professionals in banks now know the extent to which their diligence in record-keeping may be tested, and failure to provide evidence may result in having to pay a customer for losses should they occur from a delayed transaction.

Questions

1 Does your organization have appropriate records of the appointment of your AML nominated officer or equivalent, as required by local regulation?

2 Who owns AML record-keeping maintenance in your organization?

3 Records should be kept on all aspects of the decision-making process when deciding to submit an SAR, including the reasons for suspicion that confirm the state of mind of the reporter questioning the transaction as suspicious. Take a sample of your SARs submitted, asking, 'Is there sufficient detail to clearly indicate why there is suspicion?'

4 Do you think that the quality of SARs your organization has submitted to law enforcement is sufficient to enable decisions to be made by the FIU on whether the transactions in question can proceed or not?

5 Do you keep records of decisions where your organization proceeds with a transaction and what further steps have been taken to give assurance?

Stop and think

Do your contracts with customers currently contain wording that would protect your organization when: 1) there is a delay in processing a transaction because you are awaiting consent to proceed, or 2) you are pressed by a customer to disclose why you are not making the transaction?

As an AML professional you need employees to know that it is their responsibility to report suspicious activity, but they should not report on speculation alone. There must be a factual basis for making SARs; they should not be made lightly and clear records need to be kept on the reasons for the activity leading to the suspicions.

Suspicion may arise in a client relationship where an employee notices something different or unexpected that does not tally with the purpose of the relationship as declared during the client due diligence process. Concern may be triggered in the mind of the employee, and clear escalation and confidentiality expectations will help when determining the next steps. It is important once a concern is established that the employee does not let the client know either directly or by insinuation that he or she is under suspicion. Enquiries of the client by the employee can, however, be made to establish whether there is actually a suspicion. Once the employee's mind is settled that there is suspicion, taking into account the information gathered, an internal SAR should be made to the nominated officer for evaluation. As soon as the SAR is made to your local FIU, it is essential not to let the suspected party know that this has been done. This would be a clear case of tipping off.

Note

Tipping off is where, either directly or by insinuation, the suspected party is made aware that they are under suspicion. Care must be taken in the enquiry phase not to alert the client, but especially after an external SAR is made. This is when the criminal offence of tipping off could be committed, so include it as an essential part of effective AML training.

Essentially, internal reports need to get to the nominated officer quickly, and with as much information as possible. The best way to do this is open to debate. Some organizations insist on the SAR being reviewed by line management before reporting to the nominated officer; while for others, reports must have no impediments on their way to the nominated officer.

Stop and think

Is your internal SAR mechanism working efficiently, and do submitted SARs contain all relevant information by the time they get to the nominated officer? Time is of the essence and it may be that relevant employees could benefit from focused training to improve the quality of their SARs.

When developing an internal reporting mechanism for your organization, a significant factor when determining the escalation process is how many SARS are reported. Your organization may have thousands if not millions of retail customers. In this case you are likely to have sophisticated software with red flags set into transaction programming to identify activity that falls outside of the norm, as discussed in Chapter 6. The team of people who review those red flags will be able to filter out the false positives so that only internally verified issues are reported to the nominated officer for review. That same nominated officer may carry out all of the due diligence personally for, say, merger and acquisition activity, especially when dealing with high-risk countries, producing an entirely appropriate hybrid control environment.

Note

Red flag indicators are set as triggers in software systems, providing automated suspicious activity detection where relevant, and reviewed, probably by monitoring teams, before raising a concern with the nominated officer. Red flags identified by individuals in day-to-day engagement with clients may be reviewed with line management first, or be reported directly to the nominated officer.

Where an organization has a manageably small number of clients, it may be more practical for the nominated officer to review all red flags as they occur. This not only provides consistency of approach, it also provides frequent cases for the person responsible to consider, which helps to maintain competence and help in more readily recognizing suspicious patterns of activity. Whichever approach is adopted, and a hybrid approach may be best, the requirement remains the same: good quality internal reporting of suspicious activity to the nominated officer in a timely manner, to enable external reporting as quickly as possible.

Once the concern has been investigated internally, either an explanation of the activity may be found, or the concern will remain.

If the latter, it should be notified to the FIU, via an SAR. If there is difficulty in finding evidence of a person's suspicion, information gathered during initial client due diligence (CDD) may play its part. It may be, for example, that the employee checked the CDD records and found that the purpose of the relationship was inconsistent with what followed, as with Lancore Services in Case Study 6.2. With any record-keeping carried out for AML purposes, think of data gathered from the start of the client relationship as auditable records that may be called forwards to a court of law in due course.

Having said that, there are a relatively low number of successful prosecutions for money laundering in most common law jurisdictions, and in the UK an objective test of suspicion has been applied. Under POCA the objective test of suspicion requires that a prosecutor prove a person had reasonable grounds to suspect that money laundering was taking place, as in Case Study 7.1, and an offence of failure to report may be committed if it is found that this was not done. In the case of Baden v Société Générale pour Favoriser le Développement du Commerce et de l'Industrie en France SA [1993] 1WLR 509 where there was a failure to report, it was found that suspicious activity was seen but deliberately ignored, and indicators of wilful blindness to money laundering were uncovered. The concept of wilful blindness is now extended in English law to give a criminal offence of wilful blindness to bribery.

Note: Indicators of wilful blindness

- Deliberate refusal to see the obvious.
- Failing to make enquiries that a reasonable and honest person would make.
- Having knowledge of facts that indicate wrongdoing and taking no action.

Let us take a moment to consider the concept of defensive SARs. Where there is a requirement to submit SARs there may also be criminal consequences for not doing so. The tendency may then be to submit an SAR on very slight suspicion so that the nominated officer will not have to face a charge of failure to report. These SARs are unlikely to be of a good enough quality to allow a decision to be made on whether consent can be granted and they slow down the FIU's ability to respond to SARs where the speed of turnaround for consent is crucial, as in Case Study 7.1.

Note

Do not underestimate the value of records gathered during CDD and monitoring processes. They may give valuable evidence of inconsistency in the client relationship.

Competent employees who know it is their responsibility to apply the brakes at key moments, as discussed in Chapter 4, and who have been trained in how to prevent your organization being used to launder the proceeds of crime, will more readily recognize suspicious activity when it occurs. Criminals are creative, though, and new methods used to perpetrate cybercrime can fool even experienced AML professionals. In Case Study 7.2, only the unease that Matthew felt as elements of a payment request did not stack up prevented fraud and money laundering.

CASE STUDY 7.2: Invoice redirection

As manager of the compliance department at Mallards Estate Agency (MEA), Matthew was responsible for maintaining the training and software contracts relevant to his area. Each year he sourced Code of Conduct and AML online training afresh, which he tailored to the particular needs of the MEA group of companies. His choice for the current year was an old favourite, Abacus Training. It always produced very clear interactive online training, albeit with recurrent issues in its timeliness for delivery and general administration.

After the training was delivered, late as usual, Abacus Training submitted its invoice for payment. When Matthew looked at it, it was not clear to which services the invoice referred, so he let Finance know that the invoice should not be paid at the current time and queried it with his contact, Sue, at Abacus Training. Sue seemed very stressed and erratic in her e-mails, and Matthew thought he would give her a little time before responding. She was usually so clear and helpful! Wondering if it was him and not Sue that was being inconsistent, he asked team member Lesley to review the e-mails and call Sue on the telephone to see how things were. While Sue and Lesley were talking, Lesley received another e-mail from 'Sue' demanding payment for the training to be made to a new bank account. Lesley immediately asked the real Sue whether she had sent the e-mail. Answer, 'No!' and the penny dropped.

A report immediately went in to IT Security, alerting them to the issue. Upon investigation, it was found there was a hacker manipulating e-mails between Sue and Matthew, and now Lesley too. While IT Security identified the breach, Matthew obtained details of the bank account into which the hacker wanted payment to be made. Having already established good relationships with AML professionals at the bank via networking over the years, Matthew was able to quickly alert them that the account was being used to perpetrate fraud. At the bank, AML client account manager, Joseph, was able to make his own internal investigation. He found that an earlier fraud had been reported to the FIU from a person at the same address as the hacker in Matthew's case, using a different bank. Joseph then quickly moved to close the account and made his own report to the FIU. When Joseph and Matthew spoke just 90 minutes later, all necessary activity was complete to prevent further invoice diversion attempts using that route. Matthew was amazed at the speed of resolution, and very happy to be able to report a timely and successful interception of the hacker's activity to senior management.

Questions

1 How do payments to third parties get approval in your organization?

2 Do you have a mechanism by which bank account details for third parties cannot be changed without authority by the Finance department?

3 Do you provide training to employees to raise awareness of the online threats that may occur inside your company firewall?

In summary, when reporting suspicious activity the first step could well be a query or concern for which there is little further information available. Although it is not necessary to have proof or evidence of money laundering before making the report, answers to a number of key questions may help to determine whether or not it is valid. Perhaps a call to the client could provide a rationale for the activity, which can be added to your client notes. Always investigate unusual activity that gives cause for concern, and report it to your responsible officer, following your organization's procedures. Avoid submitting defensive SARs that clog up the system and give the FIU just too much data to review. You don't want to be slowing the FIU response to SARs that require a speedy turnaround for consent to avoid potential losses to a customer, as in Case Study 7.1.

So, taking the responsibility in your organization to diligently assess suspicion is a great help to the FIU in clearing away insignificant issues before they are even reported. Collaboration and respect of each other's priorities of this kind provide a positive environment in which to work with government authorities in your local jurisdiction. In the UK, for example, there are associations such as the Institute of Money Laundering Prevention Officers where AML professionals can meet, network and hear up-to-date information from regulators, government offices and the police on developments in combating financial crime locally, including external counsel interpretations of new AML regulations and cases as they occur. Having access to this external view provides a benchmark for the activities of your organization against that of others, which helps to build confidence in the adequacy of the AML controls in place in your organization.

Regulatory consequences of failures in AML controls

In an SAR to your local FIU, you may be asking for consent to proceed with a transaction. Case Study 7.1 illustrates the pitfalls that your organization may be exposed to when it does so. To improve the quality of your SARs, consider the following areas in AML controls that have repeatedly failed under scrutiny.

1 Poor governance

Senior management directors of the company who:

- Do not know enough about money laundering and its relevance to their company.

- Do not know how to structure effective risk management.
- Cannot ask the difficult questions of leaders or are not motivated to do so.
- Do not exercise accountability within the organization.
- Only accept good news reports and management information when reporting to the board.
- Do not recognize poor management information that may be outdated or of poor quality.

2 Faults in CDD

- Failure to understand the results of screening, leading to poor outcomes.
- Lack of screening capability for enhanced due diligence should further details be required.
- Access to screening software restricted to a small group of users, not available to business areas.
- Match criteria in CDD software set at levels where results provide only precise matches, or provide too many partial matches making them difficult to manage.
- Failure to keep up to date with regulatory requirements.
- Failure to implement risk-based management of CDD.
- Failure to evidence search activity leading to a lack of information for monitoring, review and disclosure to competent authorities.
- Keeping evidence by way of online links rather than documentation that will reliably be available upon request.

3 Human factors

- Dominant leadership that bears no questions being asked, leading to a sub-culture of fear in the organization.
- Fixed mental attitudes of employees who are averse to change.
- Production of passive AML board reports with sections migrated forward from year to year.

In 2016, the UK Financial Conduct Authority (FCA) published a Final Notice on its investigation into the failures of AML control activities within Sonali Bank UK, as discussed in Case Study 7.3. The web address of this Final Notice (FCA, 2016) is included in the references and further reading list at the end of this chapter, and if you only look at one piece of further reading referenced in this book, choose this one! The areas of concern noted by the UK regulator are failures that are relevant to everyone involved in AML compliance, wherever you are. This is because AML regulations for all countries originate from the Financial Action Task Force 40 Recommendations as discussed in Chapter 1, and regulatory consequence for failures of adherence clarifies the steps to be taken to comply effectively. See Case Study 7.3 for more.

> **Note**
>
> Extract from UK Financial Conduct Authority Final Notice to MLRO Steven Smith dated October 2016:
>
> > The role of MLRO is a vital one in any regulated firm. The implementation of adequate AML systems and controls requires an MLRO who takes a robust approach, ensures that AML responsibilities are understood at all levels of the organization, has sound knowledge of the controls, ensures that regular testing and monitoring is carried out, and escalates concerns appropriately to senior management.

CASE STUDY 7.3: Steven Smith, SBUK

Steven Smith was responsible for AML at Sonali Bank (SBUK), holding the post of UK Controlled Function of Money Laundering Reporting Officer (MLRO). A year before his arrival at the bank in 2011, the UK FCA found serious failings in its AML systems and controls. SBUK put in place a remediation plan to address the AML control failings that they found, and it was the responsibility of Mr Smith to act upon the findings to improve the control environment.

In December 2011, the SBUK board considered the remediation plan was complete. However, reports from externally sourced auditors showed that compliance monitoring continued to be inadequate. When FCA attention turned to

SBUK again in 2014, it found systemic failings in AML training, procedures, CDD and EDD at on-boarding and in regular monitoring activity. Mr Smith was giving the board reports that provided inappropriate assurance, indicating that AML controls were adequate when Internal Audit had produced reports highlighting serious failings. Although Mr Smith had approval from the board to hire further AML personnel, the AML function continued to be inadequately resourced to carry out appropriate activities effectively. To compound this, the AML staff handbook did not provide procedures that were adequately scoped out to give employees a clear indication of what evidence was required for CDD and EDD. Without a clear policy and procedures, AML training could not be effective as the detail of AML activity was lacking, and the scope of monitoring was unclear. Combined with the absence of carrying out branch visits that included checking AML controls, systemic weaknesses were found in the AML systems and controls of SBUK, which resulted in the FCA declaring Mr Smith to have failed the fitness and propriety test for his role. In the UK it is essential to be considered fit and proper to hold FCA Controlled Functions, and without this Mr Smith was prevented from holding the role of MLRO, negatively impacting his future career prospects.

Questions

1. Does your organization provide for carrying out EDD where required, or is there just one level of client checking?
2. Do your CDD and EDD evidencing requirements provide sufficient information on the purpose and expected activity of the relationship to enable meaningful ongoing monitoring?
3. Are your on-boarding CDD and EDD records available to compare with findings of ongoing monitoring, to ensure that the client relationship is progressing as expected?
4. Do internal auditors regularly review your AML compliance activities, and if so, how are their findings actioned and reported to the board?
5. How are failings in AML compliance activity and resourcing issues addressed in your organization?
6. Is there pressure in your organization for AML compliance to tell a good news story to the board?

Overall, in their findings on Sonali Bank, the FCA found that, 'senior management failed to ensure that SBUK fostered a culture which valued robust adherence to its regulatory responsibilities and allowed a culture of minimal, or non-compliance to persist throughout the firm'. As discussed in Chapters 2 and 3, practical policies, training and controls actively supported by senior management are the building blocks of an effective AML control environment, which were given insufficient attention by SBUK. This has a knock-on effect, as to foster a culture of compliance with regulatory responsibilities all of the elements in the AML strategy wheel (Chapter 3) work together to take on direction and commitment within an organization, and this drives cultural change towards AML regulatory understanding and adherence. Take the time to understand the cultural drivers of your organization and where they fit into the AML strategy wheel. This will give you an indication of where your attention might best be focused to take the longest strides forward with implementing a cultural shift towards AML compliance. You will find more on cultural change in Chapter 8.

Key takeaways

- FIUs gather information from SARs and other sources to inform local law enforcement agencies of financial crimes being committed.
- Whether activity is suspicious depends on individual perception. AML awareness training can greatly help to hone employee appreciation of the signs to watch out for in preventing money laundering.
- The trend from consecutive to concurrent multi-jurisdictional FIU investigations provides improved use of resources, enabling the FIUs to investigate more financial crime and money laundering cases.
- Before reporting suspicious activity to your local FIU, make sure that you have relevant information ready to provide the best details possible to assist law enforcement.
- Use records of CDD at on-boarding as reference information for ongoing monitoring teams to assess whether the client relationship is progressing as expected. This means that the on-boarding records need to be accessible, clear and contain relevant information.
- If there are issues in the AML control environment, make sure that senior management and the board are clearly informed. Good news reports won't do.

References and further reading

Barnier, M (2010) *Towards More Responsibility and Competitiveness in the European Financial Sector,* Internal Market and Services, European Commission, Brussels, p 11

Financial Conduct Authority (2016) Final Notice Sonali Bank (UK) Ltd, 12 October 2016, available from: www.fca.org.uk/publication/final-notices/sonali-bank-uk-limited-2016.pdf (last accessed 24 January 2018)

The Guardian (2017) British banks handled vast sums of laundered Russian money, available from: www.theguardian.com/world/2017/mar/20/british-banks-handled-vast-sums-of-laundered-russian-money (last accessed 24 January 2018)

Hoare, S (2005) Judge surprised by collapse of BCCI trial, *The Lawyer*, November

International Monetary Fund (2004) Financial intelligence units: an overview, available from: https:www.imf.org/external/pubs/ft/FIU/fiu.pdf (last accessed 24 January 2018)

Jayesh Shah, Shaleetha Mahabeer v HSBC Private Bank (UK) Limited [2012] EWHC 1283 (QB) (see page 18 para 67)

Kelly, C and Karmel, R S (2009) The hardening of soft law in securities regulation, *Brooklyn Journal of International Law*, **34**, p 141

Koh, H H (1997) Why do nations obey international law? *Faculty Scholarship Series,* Paper 2101

Levin, C (2012) Opening statement, US Senate Permanent Subcommittee on Investigations, Homeland Security and Governmental Affairs Committee, p 1

MONEYVAL (2013) 8. Research Report: The postponement of financial transactions and the monitoring of bank accounts, available from: https://rm.coe.int/research-report-the-postponement-of-financial-transactions-and-the-mon/168071509b (last accessed 6 February 2018)

MONEYVAL (2015) 20. Typologies report on laundering the proceeds of organised crime, available from: https://rm.coe.int/typologies-report-on-laundering-the-proceeds-of-organised-crime/168071509d (last accessed 6 February 2018)

R v Da Silva (Hilda Gondwe) [2006] EWCA Crim 1654; [2007] 1 W.L.R. 303 (see para 16)

Senden, L (2004) *Soft Law in European Community Law,* Hart Publishing, Portland, OR, p 110

Shaaban bin Hussien v Chong Fook Kam [1970] A.C. 942; [1970] W.L.R. 441 (see page 948 para B)

Walker, G A (2001) *International Banking: Law, Policy, and Practice,* Kluwer Law International, London, p 247

Navigating cultural change

08

Bearing in mind that interested countries, regulators and organizations alike are all on a journey towards eliminating corruption and money laundering, this chapter will cover:

- Cultural change at national level:
  - Cultural impact of weak regulation.
  - Strengthening regulatory adherence.
  - Cultural implications of regulatory scope-creep.
- Cultural change in organizations:
  - Cultural change management.
  - The role of policies in effecting cultural change.
  - Becoming an effective business partner.

So, why is it worth making all that effort to impede criminals laundering the proceeds of their crimes through our countries and organizations? It can be summed up no better than in the words of Kofi Annan, Secretary-General of the United Nations from January 1997 to December 2006, in his 2003 statement on the adoption by the General Assembly of the UN Convention Against Corruption. He makes clear the devastating impact of corruption on societies, especially in developing countries:

> Corruption… undermines democracy and the rule of law… and allows organized crime, terrorism and other threats… to flourish… The adoption of the United Nations Convention against Corruption sends a clear message that the international community is determined to prevent and control corruption… Corrupt officials will in future find fewer ways to hide their illicit gains. (Annan, 2003)

What a call to arms! The rationale makes clear why it is worth dedicating valuable working hours to countering the ability of criminals to use your organization through which to launder their dirty money.

Cultural impact of weak regulation

Financial services regulatory controls are aimed at the protection of consumers, combating financial crime, promoting financial stability and market integrity; efforts to achieve this by the international community acting together are gradually transcending geographical boundaries. This is beneficial as the collective approach more effectively regulates the conduct of corporate entities to encourage risk minimization, albeit on a reactive basis. However, there is a negative impact on controls when regulators are weak and regulatory arbitrage provides opportunities for criminals.

Frequently following financial scandals and other major events, developments are made to local law and regulations that strengthen both financial services and anti-money laundering (AML) controls. This happened with far-reaching effects in the case of Enron in Case Study 1.3, and again with the Bank of Credit and Commerce International (BCCI) in Case Study 8.1 where the countries involved introduced deterrents in the form of sanctions in the criminal courts, which include corporate fines and custodial sentences for money laundering offences.

CASE STUDY 8.1: Reactive regulatory reform

In the UK, BCCI was closed down by the Bank of England in July 1991 after being found engaging in several criminal activities, including fraud, tax evasion, money laundering, arms trafficking and bribery (Hoare, 2005).

This scandal resulted in a review of the Securities and Investments Board by its Chairman, Andrew Large, who produced a report (Large, 1997) recommending greater transparency in regulation and the implementation of the government's plans on regulatory reform (Walker, 2001). As a result of this the UK changed its regulatory structure from having several self-regulating organizations to the introduction of one regulator empowered by legislation: the Financial Services Authority (FSA). Upon its introduction in 2001 FSA received regulatory powers provided by the Financial Services and Markets Act 2000 (FSMA) which, incidentally, did not include financial stability. The subsequent lack of effective embedding of the controls provided by FSMA because of the reactive and political nature of regulatory development negatively impacted on their credibility. To remediate, the UK embarked on another round of regulatory reform, introducing in 2013 a 'twin peaks' model of regulation broadly covering conduct and prudential aspects separately and, being in the post-2008 financial crash era, responsibilities included financial stability. The Prudential Regulatory Authority became the prudential regulator of banks, building societies, credit unions, insurers and designated investment firms, with the Financial Conduct Authority owning prudential regulation for the remaining 18,000 regulated entities as well as conduct regulation for all 56,000 of them (FCA, 2017). Both contain elements of financial crime regulation, and have the aim of improving regulatory outcomes by providing a greater focus on each area.

Questions

1 Which model of financial services regulation is in place in your country (see the note below for a selection of the most prevalent models)?

2 Where are regulations on financial crime and money laundering located in the AML regulatory rule book in force in your country?

Note

Various regulatory models have developed locally, including:

- *Unitary:* where there is one regulator with responsibilities for conduct and prudential regulation across all sectors.
- *Twin peaks:* where conduct and prudential regulation are split between two lead regulators.
- *Sector-based regulation:* where separate regulators exist for insurance, investments, mortgage lending, etc.

Whatever the structure of the regulatory landscape, regulations devised to control behaviour can only be effective if the individuals carrying out supervision and enforcement activity are adequately skilled and knowledgeable, and can apply them consistently.

> **Note**
>
> Regulatory arbitrage is carried out by criminals and businesses when seeking out jurisdictions with weak regulatory controls and limited or no financial and corporate transparency in which to set up their operations, then implementing the minimum of organizational controls to comply with regulation, so reducing the effectiveness of the controls in a 'race to the bottom'. Countries can act as catalysts for regulatory arbitrage by not putting in place financial transparency and controls, and so draw in more business.

Poor delivery of enforcement results is clearly detrimental to a regulator's credibility. Regulated industries and criminals alike recognize it, and look for inconsistencies that weaken the effect of regulation, which is of no help at all to compliance leaders when introducing AML controls into an organization.

> **Note**
>
> Macro-prudential risks are those that can build up in the financial system internationally. The actions of multiple country regulators are required to better manage these, hence the importance of the Financial Action Task Force (FATF) and other standard-setting bodies, as discussed in Chapter 1. Micro-prudential risks are the more granular risks that local rules and enforcement are put in place to control.

The rules country regulators make, their supervision of compliance with those rules, enforcement where they find non-compliance, and litigation when the rules are broken are micro-prudential in nature. Rules are important, but they do not mitigate macro-prudential risks that can build up in the financial system, such as those that remained unnoticed in the lead up to the financial crisis of 2008. They were not sufficiently recognized by the international community to enable effective regulation, which demonstrated that operating with local micro-prudential regulation was not enough.

However, using jurisdictional hard law alone it was shown to be impossible to embed effective regulation including AML controls in an organization without embracing the international soft law conventions provided by standard-setting bodies. These may be considered as impaired as they are non-enforceable, and in theory they can be completely overlooked. However, taking the example of FATF as discussed in Chapter 1, they are important influencers of corporates and governments alike, as they have acquired 'meaning, significance and legal status' (Senden, 2004).

Note

Operating models can be centralized: where control of regulatory adherence is held at head office, with branches and subsidiaries reporting to a central point of governance; or decentralized: where the branches and subsidiaries themselves manage regulatory adherence without, or with minimal guidance from head office.

Weak regulation is exacerbated with a decentralized operating model and where the systems and controls of international enterprise blur the bright lines of territorial control. Also, when a multinational enterprise is doing business in a developing jurisdiction it might seek to benefit from regulatory arbitrage, taking the course of least regulation, which can lower the threshold of the whole organization to sub-standard practices. Equally, those international entities need to be mindful that they will be judged by the standards of their most heavily regulated jurisdiction.

Take the case of the Hong Kong and Shanghai Bank (HSBC) and its stance on money laundering risk in Case Study 8.2. Over several years, HSBC assured US regulators that it was taking the risk of money laundering very seriously, while its activities ultimately were shown to be actively facilitating money laundering on an institutional basis.

CASE STUDY 8.2: HSBC Mexico

HSBC operated a decentralized model, with subsidiary entities looking after their own local regulatory requirements and little if no oversight of these activities from their London head office. One thing head office did specify, however, was that the locally based Responsible Officers for AML take on the HSBC view of money laundering risk. So, what's the problem, I hear you ask. Well, the problem was that HSBC had a very individual method of assessing money laundering risk, which had the effect of facilitating money laundering on a grand scale.

This is the position HSBC found itself in when its decentralized management model, focusing on local country leaders, did not allow international AML policies and procedures to be adequately implemented. It ignored the Transparency International Risk Perceptions Index, and allocated lower risk levels with accompanying lighter touch AML controls in countries of higher risk, which enabled the money laundering to happen. This resulted in action against HSBC in the United States for allowing drugs money from Mexico to be laundered easily through its business (Levin, 2012). HSBC found that while its old model served it well historically, before financial globalization, 'it does not work in an interconnected world where transactions cross borders instantaneously and where weaknesses in one jurisdiction can be quickly exported to others' (Levin, 2012).

The effect of weak regulatory response and action on HSBC's activity in establishing effective AML organizational controls in Mexico was eventually highlighted in 2012 when its choice of strategy and assessment of money laundering risk was revealed to the US Senate Subcommittee for Investigations. Rather than relying on the collective requirements of international bodies and applying a standard that satisfied the soft law international codes, HSBC operated its subsidiary network by exploiting the advantages of regulatory arbitrage, only being exposed for money laundering when it came to the attention of the regulator from a neighbouring state. HSBC was found to have operated an indefensible analysis of AML risk in its jurisdictions, products and services. The in-house AML risk assessment placed Mexico, standing at 100 out of 183 countries on the Transparency International Corruption Perceptions Index 2011, as 'low risk' for anti-money laundering controls, at the same time as HSBC was allowing billions of US dollars of drugs money to be laundered from Mexico through its US outlets while 'playing fast and loose with US banking rules' (Levin, 2012). Here both the board and management, who were aware of the rules covering AML in the United States, required affiliates not to carry out their own due diligence on the potential risks of transactions, but to accept the 'low risk' classification as applied by the head office. This active failure of HSBC to control the risk of being used as a vehicle through which to launder the proceeds of crime and actually to enable it, continued for a number of years.

During this time HSBC had the attention of US regulators regarding its operations in the United States and Mexico: in 2003 HSBC was in enforcement with the Federal Reserve and the New York State Banking Department to improve its AML arrangements. This finished in 2006, but by 2010 HSBC was in enforcement once again with the Office of the Comptroller of the Currency (OCC), and was served with a Cease and Desist order requiring a second revamp of its US AML programme. In addition to this, it was found that HSBC in the United States 'stripped out or omitted any reference to Iran' (Levin, 2012) from paperwork, so circumventing requirements of the US Treasury Department's Office of Foreign Assets Control, and the Mexican entity of HSBC was prevented by US regulators in 2008 from taking large sums of physical US dollars. This catalogue of HSBC's failure to comply with AML and CTF requirements was in part enabled by the OCC's failure of AML oversight of HSBC in the United States, when it 'tolerated the mounting AML problems... for five years, without taking any formal or informal enforcement action' (Levin, 2012).

Questions

1 Does your organization have a centralized or decentralized operating model?
2 How are the level of AML risks and controls determined in your organization? Do you use international benchmarks as a guide?
3 Looking at local enforcement action, do you think that the AML controls of your organization are sufficient to withstand a regulatory investigation?

In Case Study 8.2, HSBC effectively circumvented AML regulatory controls for several years, and weakness on the part of the OCC allowed HSBC to manoeuvre around regulatory requirements, doubtless making healthy profits in its illegal money laundering operations. Perhaps HSBC would have benefited from better oversight and stronger regulatory sanction at an early stage; it may then have paid more attention to establishing effective AML regulatory controls and less to profit maximization.

Strengthening regulatory adherence

In some jurisdictions, AML regulatory requirements often become 'gold plated' and implemented as soon as possible. In the world's major financial centres the AML culture of adherence is there to give confidence to financial services customers that their funds will be well protected. More and more countries compete in the race for international business, including China, preparing for a visit from FATF, as discussed in Case Study 8.3.

CASE STUDY 8.3: Strengthening regulatory controls in China

China's President, Xi Jinping, cracked down on corruption in China during his presidency, but in the wake of the Panama Papers scandal of 2016, Hong Kong was shown to be the world's most active financial centre for the creation of shell companies. (For more on shell companies, see Chapter 6.) Of course, shell companies can be used as perfectly legitimate financial entities, but they are also known to be a favourite vehicle for money launderers. Some of the entities mentioned in the Panama Papers scandal were linked to prominent Chinese politicians, causing President Xi Jinping potential embarrassment in the lead up to FATF's visit to China in 2018.

In preparation for the FATF visit, China increased the focus of its regulatory reform to more actively implement controls to satisfy the FATF 40 Recommendations as revised in 2012 (see Table 1.1). The Financial Services and Treasury Bureau (FSTB) of Hong Kong published proposals in January 2017 to extend the reach of AML regulation to trust and company agents, lawyers, accountants and real estate agents, to have them declare the ultimate beneficial owner UBO of the business, and carry out CDD checks on clients including the source of their funds. The new licensing regime will catch the trusts and shell companies that could be laundering money, and Reuters (Price, 2017) reported that the new disclosure laws in Hong Kong may 'lead to the exodus of billions of dollars in assets from the territory as people seek to avoid increased scrutiny'. No point in moving Chinese assets to Hong Kong to escape Xi Jinping's AML activity, then!

Further activity on strengthening regulatory control before the FATF visit came from the China Banking Regulatory Commission (CBRC) also in January 2017, when it issued a guideline for Chinese banks that carry out business internationally to standardize services to comply with international norms and tighten their risk controls. In particular, the CBRC requires Chinese banks to:

> reinforce the construction of compliance systems, intensify everyday compliance management and efforts against money laundering and the financing of terrorism, allocate more resources to compliance and improve their efficiency of communications with local regulators. (Jiang, 2017)

FATF Mutual Evaluation Reports are a valuable resource when assessing the relative compliance of a country to money laundering regulation. You may find it useful to research the answers to the following questions and utilize that information in your role.

Questions

1. When was the last FATF mutual evaluation visit to your country?
2. What were the recommendations at that time?
3. Have the recommendations been implemented into the AML regulations of your country?

Cultural implications of regulatory scope-creep

The reach of AML regulation is stretching ever further, and in those organizations that are newly caught in its net there may be a resentful attitude towards compliance that results in resistance. A newly designated AML officer or employee of the company may find themselves on a lonely mission to find out about the regulations with little assistance or interest from senior management. How to navigate that and survive in the role?

There is some commentary that illustrates it can be challenging to survive in role as an AML compliance professional in certain jurisdictions. For example, in Trade Arabia's report on the inaugural Middle East and North Africa (MENA) Regulatory Summit in 2017, compliance and AML professionals in the region are:

> Seeking placements where there is active and visible support for the compliance function... compliance personnel are choosing to work for

> a company where their input will be valued and they are not at risk of losing their positions because they are in constant conflict with senior management. (Trade Arabia, 2017)

The summit was held under the patronage of the United Arab Emirates' Minister of Economy, Sultan bin Saeed Al Mansouri and in association with the Dubai Financial Services Authority. In his opening address the governor of the Dubai International Financial Centre (DIFC) introduced the summit attendees to the FinTech Hive at the DIFC, the aim of which is to bring cutting-edge financial services technology to the MENA region, and channel those technologies into a responsible and well-functioning financial services system.

An indication of how far the MENA region has travelled in its quest to implement AML controls in its organizations was reported at the same event by Thomson Reuters' Managing Director of MENA, Dadim Najjar, when he said: 'The integration of financial crime compliance into the broader business function (of an organization) is absolutely necessary, rather than simply being a nice to have.' He went on to talk about the difficulties experienced by AML professionals when attempting to implement an AML compliance regime into their organizations. For an international centre in 2017 this may be surprising, but the role of the compliance officer being described as requiring the ability to learn quickly and perform under pressure, having critical thinking and highly evolved interpersonal abilities, resonates well in the AML landscape of rapid technological, political and regulatory change. This is all in the quest to help reduce operational risks.

Dadim Najjar suggests having the character to manage senior leadership is the most essential string to the bow of the AML compliance professional. Really? Personally managing senior leadership being essential to the role? Certainly! A voice of experience from one who needed to keep their role in AML compliance may provide some insight. Senior leadership, whether or not they come from authoritarian regimes, require employees to respect their authority. Wise to keep your glass half full all the time with the optimism that it may be filled with achievements. Senior leadership like achievements, so make it your business to research really thoroughly the specific law and regulations, their purpose and the business areas they affect.

Even when you have done this, those more senior to you may not appreciate your diligence.

Cultural change often excites resistance, so start small and garner the fruits that are in reach with enthusiastic grace. As a knowledgeable AML professional, you do not have to always accept that the great and the good in an organization do actually have AML risks under appropriate management. Quite often, new regulatory demands are placed upon those people with sufficient seniority to be at the helm as figureheads, without any further attention being paid to them or their risk management. Simply having the authority to be a credible figure in the eyes of onlookers external to the organization can be deemed to be enough to 'deal with' the inconvenience of AML compliance, as Luke found in Case Study 8.4.

CASE STUDY 8.4: Attention to AML responsibilities

Imagine this. Luke, an AML compliance professional, starts his role in a global financial partnership, and introduces himself to the company's Chief Executive Officer (CEO) on his first morning. The CEO invites Luke to a meeting later in the week to discuss compliance and AML activities in the organization. Having had no handover from the previous incumbent, and being a one-person compliance department, Luke starts to review the compliance files to research his new role. Where better to start than the Annual AML Compliance Report? The previous year's report read well: all good, with expected progress. What did AML compliance do the year before? Oh, wait a minute. Comparing the reports, they were word for word and page for page the same, apart from the date on the front. For three years the previous Compliance Manager had churned out the same report and, crucially, the CEO, who held the UK Financial Conduct Authority (FCA) Controlled Function (CF) 11, Money Laundering Reporting Officer (MLRO), had not noticed.

Here is the dilemma. The MLRO was CEO of the company without AML knowledge, depending on a subordinate manager to carry out the work with insufficient oversight. The manager knew that the CEO had no interest in AML compliance, but merely held the Controlled Function because regulations required it. The CEO could now be seen to have abrogated his responsibility on AML, leaving the organization widely exposed to being used to launder the proceeds of crime, and Luke, as the new AML compliance manager, needed to tell him this was the case. Difficult. What to do before the Friday meeting was now an urgent and very important matter for Luke; he had to objectively and clearly set out the AML risks and exposure of the organization while battening down the hatches in readiness for potentially stormy seas.

Calmness in the delivery of this news was only possible for Luke in his new role because, first, he had a strong grasp of the regulatory subject, knowing how it was applicable to the activities of the organization; and secondly, because he had used almost his whole week to thoroughly research the departmental records, requesting assistance from existing employees to verify there was nothing else known there to find. Geared up with this information, Luke met with the CEO. On presenting the findings, the CEO immediately summoned his Personal Assistant (PA) to present his own files with the 'correct' information, only to find that his new recruit was right. What an annoying subordinate! Suitably rattled, the CEO immediately realized his failure in oversight and Luke, while feeling very vulnerable as to what might happen, began to suggest ways in which matters could be remedied and the risk of the organization lowered by setting out an AML compliance plan in summary form.

What would the CEO like to happen next? Would he like to carry on as MLRO, or would he like Luke to take this responsibility on for him, and report to him at regular intervals on the de-risking progress? The latter, please, came the reply, and within weeks Luke was MLRO, formally recognized and holding the Controlled Function with the FCA. Phew, and hurray together! Immediately the work of de-risking the organization's AML exposure began.

Sometimes, busy senior people who are used to holding high office do not appreciate what that office entails. Regulators may look to impose competency requirements on Controlled Function holders, such as the FCA's Senior Managers and Certification Regime 2018, but at the time, for Luke as subordinate employee, the plot was to strengthen and renew AML controls while retaining his new job, proving his worth, and settling himself in to steer the course of the organization into less risky waters as a knowledgeable MLRO.

Questions

1. Does the AML regulatory regime in your jurisdiction require Controlled Function holders to prove their competence?
2. Does AML Compliance prepare an annual board report, and if so does it reflect the activities of the year?

Cultural change is not just about making an organization implement new systems and controls to satisfy new or revised legislation, it is about bringing the organization along with you to support the change and see its value to the business. Luke's navigation of a tricky situation with his superior in Case Study 8.4 was a masterstroke of influencing skills built on subject knowledge, industry experience and regulatory awareness. It was the foundation of their long and productive professional relationship that over time helped to better manage AML risk and keep senior leadership updated and on board with changes to the AML compliance controls in their global company.

Cultural change management

Taking on the role as an agent for change in reducing the AML risk in an organization brings with it all the inherent risks of disrupting those that benefit from the status quo, and so are averse to change. These powerful elements, maybe seeming as strong as the forces of nature, can, in sailing terms, change the environment from a relaxed sail on a sunny day, to one of immediate action by the crew when a violent squall arrives. As strong gusts tip the boat on a rakish angle, the crew become immediately dependent upon each other, now trapped at sea in a vessel that may break with devastating results if poorly managed. Depending on each other's ability to use knowledge and skills well, an effective crew trims the sails tight as the boat drives forward into the oncoming wind and perches over the yacht's angled side to provide the boat with empowering balance. Knowing that everyone is contributing to the speed of progress, the crew relish in the exhilaration of successfully channelling power. This is an ideal situation, of course, and the crew that is not competent may well fail to manage the power of the wind and waves, in the same way as the AML culture in your organization will either succeed or fail when presented with significant challenge. With cultural change, when establishing or enhancing an effective AML control environment, the disruption caused by accompanying 'gusts of wind' affecting senior people, can also change the environment from one of comfort and ease to one of demanding action with far-reaching effects. In this scenario, you'll be glad that you paid attention to the role profiles of your AML team, their training and effective performance management (as discussed in Chapter 2) as now you know your team and can be confident in their abilities.

Sailors and AML professionals alike know themselves and their colleagues better after a time of pressure or challenge where every action counts. In the sailing world it can be immediately clear that if everyone is in the right place on the boat, maximizing their input to its performance, it goes faster and more smoothly through the water. With AML compliance the results of change can be slow to see and paint a less compelling picture for those who need to embrace it. Indeed, evolution rather than revolution is a mantra that I keep as my goal in terms of cultural change, as it moderates the pace to more manageable levels so causing less challenges to be placed on the individuals making up the 'crew'. Your care in providing a clear route map with your AML policy drafting and dissemination will give the whole organization a reliable basis on which to mould activity.

The role of policies in effecting cultural change

Well-written policies provide access to the risk management framework of your organization, and they are the lifeblood of your AML control environment, as discussed in Chapter 2. Keep them up to date so that no one can tell you they are dry and crusty! Elements that improve policy recognition and minimize organizational risk, as with all compliance policies, include:

- *Tone from the top:* senior management engagement in launch and practical application.
- *Expression of intent:* they embody the cultural expectations of the organization.
- *Legislative adherence:* compliance with international best practice, with the caveat that the global policy can be trumped by local laws.
- *Risk-based approach:* they define the approach and determine controls.

- *Employee behaviour:* they indicate employee duties and responsibilities.
- *Identification and verification:* checking standards and procedures clearly articulated.
- *Management information:* data gathered from the day-to-day running of procedures provides regular and objective management information.

Becoming an effective business partner

A less exciting but perhaps more reliable way of navigating cultural change is to develop the classic traits of an effective and reliable business partner. Gone are the days of 'ivory tower' AML compliance, where policies and procedures were there to be pillars of the corporate society but not necessarily implemented into business practice. Today we need to be active and visible assets to the corporate journey to be truly effective in our role.

The board, via internal and external subject-matter experts, articulates the direction for company operations by the introduction of policies, including those for the purpose of financial crime awareness and prevention. The more accessible the language in them, the more colleagues will be able to read and understand them, so the first step in becoming a business partner is to write your AML policies clearly, with an indication of the processes and procedures that are in place to guide adherence to them. Where they are held on the organization's intranet, provide a click-through to relevant procedures so readers can easily navigate to the information they need. In the maintenance and application of those policies, ensure that, as control activities are introduced, the policies are promptly updated to reflect them. It is easy to appear out of touch with the business if AML compliance policies are not kept current, and this includes ensuring they reflect the latest branding colours and images of your organization.

Policies have a tendency to tell people what to do, and whereas you may know precisely what they have to do to comply with anti-bribery and corruption (ABC) and AML requirements, being a business partner means understanding the business areas inside out before engaging with the relevant leaders and managers to implement your policy. Also, using the language of facilitation rather than of control helps when encouraging engagement; some examples are set out in Table 8.1.

Table 8.1 Language of facilitation and control

Facilitation	Control
I will help you to…	You must…
We can achieve this deadline together by…	You will achieve the deadline by…
The ways I can move this forward are…	What you have to do is…
Let us discuss and agree the revised due diligence process…	Your due diligence process is inadequate and will be replaced by…
If it would help, the AML team can partner with your delegated resource to…	My team is going to implement this process and tell your team how to administer it…

For an AML professional to make progress in implementing new processes, it is essential to have honed your competent AML team to reach out and influence business leaders and network with other governance functions to understand their needs. Using this approach, AML controls can better complement existing functions and add value to the whole organization. The ability to influence involves gaining the respect of those to be influenced, so ensure you have an excellent grasp of your own subject, and closely study the area of the business that needs to change. Even where implementing legally required AML controls, a positive approach of, 'How can I help you to implement this new requirement into your already successful area?' is likely to gain more support than, 'What a mess! You clearly need me to sort this out for you.' AML professionals need a strategy to encourage business areas to engage with reducing their operational risk, and keeping the 'sea' calm with benign winds will ensure the AML 'boat' is moving along just fine, but with little disruption to the business area and smoother progress.

Working together with stakeholders in this way to agree a way forward may be a little slow at times, but it is likely to produce longer-lasting positive results than to satisfy the ego by imposing a solution.

This sacrifice of expediency is to the greater good of establishing the value that AML compliance can bring to the business. Building up your value-added positive capital will help when you have difficult messages or requests as they are better received when they come from a trusted adviser than from a distant compliance officer who knows little about the affected business area. Knowledge of the business areas or functions you support will also demonstrate that you have the best interests of your organization at heart, and if your relationship with leaders in your organization includes asking how you can help them to achieve their business objectives, then their engagement with AML compliance will gain momentum towards improvement.

AML leaders, albeit at team or company level, need to develop a management style or plan that will contribute to an improved AML compliance culture over time, and holding constructive expectations is a hugely positive stance in managing organizational processes through change. Combine that with managing conflicts constructively and you will lead AML compliance towards sustainable effectiveness for employees, the team and the organization as a whole. Managing for success will include taking on challenging tasks, objectively analysing their elements, and drawing in all stakeholders as valued contributors by treating the people involved with respect and consideration. This applies even if they are active detractors in the beginning, as Clare found out in Case Study 8.5. Give them the opportunity to embrace the change despite their reservations and they could turn round to be your greatest supporters.

CASE STUDY 8.5: Managing headwinds

AML manager, Clare, was tasked with travelling to Japan as AML and ABC Ambassador of the organization, armed with a presentation she had researched herself. She knew exactly what it contained and why, and so would be able to explain and/or defend its contents should she be called upon to do so. Clare ensured before her visit that the content was accurate in legal terms, and that it had the active support of senior management. She knew that her first two days would be spent on training, followed by an audit of the AML controls.

Clare arrived in Tokyo and Chikoyo showed her to her office, positioned between the Country Manager, Makoto, and the Regional Leader, Cedric. Both were aware of her visit and its purpose, and the largest meeting room was booked for two sessions of the mandatory AML and ABC training that day. On hearing her arrival, Cedric summoned Chikoyo to his office and began a rant against his team wasting their time on the training, so loud that the whole office could hear – including Clare and Makoto. When it stopped, Clare, smiling and calm, walked out into the open office space and seeing that Cedric's door was open, she went in, greeting him with outstretched hand: 'Cedric! So good to meet you in person! It's always good to receive a warm welcome when I've travelled so far.' She totally disarmed him. Cedric was not expecting the instant and complete nullification of his excessive objection, and Clare was able to set out the objectives of her visit and the relevance of the training to his team, while navigating his effusive apology. The net result of this was Cedric's unswerving support of the training. He sent out a communication to his whole team that the training was mandatory and they must all attend, which they did, signing in upon arrival.

Afterwards, Clare asked Makoto, the Country Manager, for feedback on the training session. Makoto thanked her first for raising the awareness of AML and ABC in the region as he was struggling to make people understand that they really did have to acknowledge and comply with the company processes to prevent money laundering and bribery. (Cedric's behaviour was testament to that!) He then paused, and looking with new respect at the person who had defeated Cedric's objections, he said something that would stay with her throughout her career: 'and the authority, of your (training presentation) delivery, was perfect'. He then sought Clare's guidance on the appointment of a dedicated resource to ensure that the AML policies and procedures were observed, and assured her of Japan's active support in her AML and ABC efforts for the organization. The strength of character she had demonstrated in her treatment of Cedric gave Makoto the confidence to nominate an employee in the knowledge that they would receive strong support from head office to withstand future 'Cedric moments'.

Questions

1 Do your trainers receive sufficient training themselves in the subject matter of their presentations to answer most queries raised when they deliver presentations?

2 When preparing for country visits, do you provide your AML professionals with coaching on the handling of objections?

3 What is the proportion of training delivered in your organization between online and face-to-face?

Be the rising tide of AML compliance culture in your business: the knowledgeable and inclusive source of de-risking information and guidance that your organization needs.

Key takeaways

- Weak regulation in a jurisdiction tends to encourage the implementation of weak regulatory controls in organizations too, and combined they can form a seemingly acceptable modus operandi. The culture this encourages can be one of regulatory arbitrage, a race to the bottom of adherence to law and regulation in favour of minimizing regulatory intervention in business operations.
- Strengthening regulatory adherence can be seen in jurisdictions where there is a desire to interact more fully on the international stage. The activity of Xi Jinping in China (see Case Study 8.3) is an example of this.
- The cultural implications of AML regulatory scope-creep include senior management of newly regulated organizations tending to give the requirements insufficient importance. This can result in a lack of attention to regulatory requirements by AML employees themselves, whether because of lack of guidance or an inclination to neglect. An engaged tone from the top early on helps the drive towards AML compliance.
- Cultural change is inherently disruptive, so finding the right pace in your organization by which to implement evolving AML controls is essential. The more you can do with the greatest buy-in from senior management and the least disruption to the business will provide you with a path of fewer impediments and greater progress.
- Policies are very useful in effecting cultural change as long as they are clear, provide sufficient guidance and your organization actually does require employees to abide by them. Where policies are in place but ignored in day-to-day operations, compliance and AML professionals alike have difficulties in embedding the controls necessary to prevent your organization being an easy target for money launderers.
- Becoming an effective business partner enhances the value of AML compliance to the organization. Seek to move the organizational agenda forward with the management of AML controls and see your profile within the business improve.

References and further reading

Annan, K (2003) The Secretary-General: Statement On The Adoption By The General Assembly Of The United Nations Convention Against Corruption 31/10. United Nations Office on Drugs and Crime, New York, available from: www.unodc.org/unodc/en/treaties/CAC/background/secretary-general-speech.html (last accessed 7 February 2018)

Block, A (2001) *The Organised Criminal Activities of the Bank of Credit and Commerce International: Essays and documentation*, Springer Science & Business Media, Dordrecht

Culture AMP (No Date) 11 Essential Traits of Great Managers, available from: http://hello.cultureamp.com/hubfs/1702-Essential-Traits/11-Essential-Traits-of-Great-Managers.pdf (last accessed 7 February 2018)

Financial Action Task Force (2018) Publications, Mutual Evaluations, available from: http://www.fatf-gafi.org/publications/mutualevaluations/?hf=10&b=0&s=desc(fatf_releasedate) (last accessed 7 February 2018)

Financial Conduct Authority (2017) CP17/40: Individual accountability: Transitioning FCA firms and individuals to the Senior Managers & Certification Regime, available from: https://www.fca.org.uk/publications/consultation-papers/cp17-40-individual-accountability-transitioning-fca-firms-and-individuals-senior-manager (last accessed 8 February 2018)

Hoare, S (2005) Judge Surprised by Collapse of BCCI Trial, *The Lawyer* 3/11

Jiang, X (2017) Bank focuses more on compliance risk control 14/2, *China Daily*, available from: www.chinadaily.com.cn/business/2017-02/14/content_28192824.htm (last accessed 7 February 2018)

Large, A (1997) Report to the Chancellor on the Reform of the Financial Regulatory System (The Large Report), London

Levin, C (2012) Opening statement, *US Vulnerabilities to Money Laundering, Drugs and Terrorist Financing: HSBC case history*, US Senate Permanent Subcommittee on Investigations, Homeland Security and Governmental Affairs Committee (July)

Perkins, D and Zimmerman, A (1995) Empowerment theory, research, and application, *American Journal of Community Psychology*, **23** (5), p 569

Price, M (2017) Hong Kong takes aim at middlemen in wake of Panama Papers scandal 14/2. Reuters Business News, available from: https://uk.reuters.com/article/uk-hongkong-regulations-moneylaundering/hong-kong-takes-aim-at-middlemen-in-wake-of-panama-papers-scandal-idUKKBN15T33B (last accessed 7 February 2018)

Senden, L (2004) *Soft Law in European Community Law*, Hart Publishing, Portland, OR

Thomson Reuters, Deloitte (2017) Financial Crime in the Middle East and North Africa 2017: The Need for Forward Planning, available from: https://mena.thomsonreuters.com/content/dam/openweb/documents/pdf/mena/report/mena-financial-crime-report-2017.PDF (last accessed 8 February 2018)

Trade Arabia (2017) Many officers 'lack confidence in AML programmes' 6/2, available from: http://www.tradearabia.com/news/BANK_320275.html (last accessed 8 February 2018)

US v BCCI Holdings (Luxembourg) SA et al., 1991 Crim. No. 91–0655 (JHB)

Walker, G A (2001) *International Banking: Law, policy and practice*, Kluwer Law International, London, p 247

Conclusion

This book has explored money laundering from several angles to expand on just what it is, and how it affects the work and activity of risk management professionals in the area of anti-money laundering (AML) and how this risk can be managed to benefit the business. Starting with the interest of members of the Organization for Economic Co-operation and Development (OECD) keen to rid their countries of drug money, the Financial Action Task Force (FATF) introduced modern-day AML regulations, which grew up to minimize the risk of organizations being used as vehicles through which the proceeds of crime could be laundered. Together with introducing risk-based AML operational controls, we have considered how cultural change gradually comes into effect as governance measures and regulations bite.

In summary, the book has set out information and guidance as follows:

- Regulatory progression.
- Policies and procedures.
- Training.
- Using the AML strategy wheel.
- Identifying failures of the AML control framework.
- Why AML transparency is king on the international stage.
- Client due diligence in risk assessment.
- Advantages and disadvantages of weak or strong regulators.
- Navigating cultural change when implementing your AML strategy.

Regulatory progression

Regulatory progression describes the progress that governments have made in assisting AML professionals implement a control environment into their organizations to prevent them being used as a vehicle for use by criminals in laundering the proceeds of their crimes; they have done this by building the regulatory framework. By charting progression in AML regulatory development in the early days, one can see OECD countries collaborate to form the FATF with their efforts focused on a known peril: the use by criminals of organizations in their countries to traffick drugs. Then, with the advent of the internet, came the vastly accelerated pace of online transaction capability, testing the collaborative progress of Financial Intelligence Units (FIUs) in spotting and intercepting the movement of funds. Terrorist activity also encouraged a regulatory response, and as a result of the 11 September 2001 terrorist attacks on the World Trade Center in New York, the FATF introduced its Special Recommendations to counter terrorist financing.

Regulatory progression is inherently retrospective as the regulators respond to new criminal activities and the egregious situations that arise. This is especially the case in rules-based regulatory regimes where changing regulations can be a slow process. Principles-based regulation eases the situation as the principles overarch the rules to provide statements of intent on which the regulators can base decisions in monitoring and enforcement. However, in principles-based regulation there is the expectation that the guiding minds of obliged entities will adhere to the code of principles of the regulator, and when this does not happen, the model faces challenges. Maintaining a rule book for surety of guidance with an overlay of principles was the approach taken by the UK's Financial Services Authority in the early 2000s in a move towards introducing flexibility in regulation that ultimately proved to be less than effective. The most forward-looking regulatory environment is where the rulebook has an overlay of guiding principles, but where regulatory powers focus on imposing sanctions on obliged entities when their activities fall outside of acceptable principles. Outcomes-based regulation provides the most flexible environment in which obliged entities can operate as it gives them the freedom to design products and services as they wish. Control of the outcomes to customers and those depending on the services is put into effect again by regulatory oversight and enforcement activity.

> **Note**
>
> Wherever in the world your organization is located, look to FATF guidance together with the AML laws and regulations of your country to assess readiness for international trade.

Policies and procedures

Taking the time to produce your AML policies and procedures as narrative guidance for your organization helps to minimize organizational risks (see Chapter 5 for more). The stable environment of well-written policies enables focus to be applied to emerging risks, the management of which can itself then become part of policy making and procedural management.

It is less time-consuming to buy in policies from external providers, of course, and their content is highly likely to satisfy legal requirements, but doing so will not develop knowledge and skills within your organization. Better to write practical, clear and succinct guidance that is tailored specifically for your organization then have it checked by external counsel. In this way the policy writer and team will know that they have all the relevant organizational aspects covered, and that they are legally sound. If the lawyers find an error or omission, all to the good as the policy writer will be better informed for next time. The results of policy implementation together with documented procedures within the risk control environment will better enable a holistic view where money laundering risks occur, and more readily form part of the wider business reporting to senior leadership.

Training

In the same way as taking the time to produce tailored policies for your organization will pay dividends, producing training that is 100 per cent relevant to employees within your area of regulation gives an indicator of your engagement with and knowledge of the risks your organization has to manage. If you do not have the resources to produce this in-house, there are training providers out there that can take your policies and procedures and produce the levels of training modules you need to cover your AML risks, but at a price. Depending on the AML knowledge and skills already in your organization, the judgement will be yours to mitigate the risk of failing to provide adequate training to employees. This is of prime importance, as in many jurisdictions there are legal requirements upon the AML Responsible Officer (RO) to train employees to a level of competence and keep records of this training to prove diligence. Where this is not carried out there can be legal consequences for the AML RO, including jail time. This is clearly to be avoided!

From a knowledge and skills perspective, for employees to determine that an activity is suspicious, they first need to understand what acceptable activity looks like. They need training to be aware of the indicators of suspicious activity in your industry to enable them to spot the difference between acceptable and unacceptable behaviour. Using a tailored focus for your training will provide guidance to employees which they will recognize as being relevant to them. Spend time on getting this right, as in my experience this is a key component to employee engagement. Once the training is established, working on updates to the training with employees in the relevant business area if an additional suspicious activity is recognized, will further encourage their vigilance in spotting suspicious activity as it arises. Taking opportunities where you find them to work with employees to better implement a robust and effective AML risk control framework for your organization will pay dividends.

Using the AML strategy wheel

The AML strategy wheel articulates the wealth of activity that makes up AML risk management, separating out the elements for allocation to team members while providing an indication of the linkages that will be necessary between the elements to effectively collaborate in reducing organizational risk. It also gives indicators as to how the different smaller wheels feed into the overall activity of AML risk management. None of them can function effectively in isolation, as discussed in Chapter 3. Policies, procedures, training, controls – each area of the AML strategy wheel gives the opportunity to influence the leaders of your organization in a positive way. A mantra in my team, even when it is difficult to achieve, is to positively influence business area team members and leaders alike with each contact.

AML professionals need leaders to take ownership of organizational risk, and as they will probably need encouragement to do so it is useful to be able to articulate your plan in a clear and succinct way. Encouragement to senior managers to take individual accountability for the risks they manage is being provided by the UK regulator with its Senior Managers and Certification Regime, as a replacement for the Approved Persons regime. This change came about following the 2008 financial crisis, when the UK Parliamentary Commission for Banking Standards recommended the introduction of an accountability framework focused on senior management, which includes Statements of Responsibilities. This forward-looking study into mapping of responsibilities by risk is a useful resource in assessing organizational risk, whether or not its activities fall inside the regulatory regime.

Once your risk-based AML control environment is in place and working, the major part of what to include and why will have already been agreed, and testing of the control framework with each of the individual elements can commence. Testing the elements for relevance and effectiveness is ongoing and forms part of usual activity within AML compliance. The policies and procedures will need to be updated within an agreed revision cycle, and elements that at first iteration were unclear or omitted can be corrected to provide an improved version. Should Internal Audit make an assessment of your AML controls, whether it finds them adequate or not, review them with reference to regulatory sanctions on individuals and organizations in your jurisdiction. If there is nothing relevant locally, look further afield: the foundations of AML regulation are the same for all and, ultimately, a recognized failure in one jurisdiction provides guidance on what is expected in others, which is particularly true for companies operating internationally.

> **Note**
>
> With each contact, seek to positively influence your stakeholders by showcasing the benefits to them of engagement with AML risk management.

Identifying failures of the AML control framework

This work is never ending! There are always residual risks when implementing a risk management control framework and AML is no different. It is tempting to focus too much attention on implementing preventive points in the control environment at the expense of risk identification points. No manager wants to have a risk control failure identified on his or her watch, but in automated systems risk alerts or 'red flags' set at levels of transaction or currency requested can provide valuable raw material for review of where heightened risk is identified. Where operating in automated data processing systems, these red flag risk indicators are only going to work if they are set to actually identify current and relevant risks, so they should be under constant surveillance in a flexible system. If you are not careful enough to keep the red flag indicators current, they can quickly become irrelevant, leading to a failure of your AML control framework. If the transactions of your organization are monitored manually, there is the advantage of human judgement and observation to readily identify high-risk transactions, but also the risk of human error, deliberate obscuring of data or lack of diligence to factor in.

Moving to management and the boardroom, there is no point in filtering reports to provide only good news on AML controls. Arguably the biggest failure of the AML control framework is to have the organization's guiding minds lulled into a false sense of security that all the risks of being used as a vehicle for money launderers are well under control. As in Case Study 7.3, this may not end well, as the reality is that the money launderers do care about cleaning their dirty money, and obliged entities need to build risk management into their operating model.

> **Note**
>
> Seek out potential failures of your AML control framework in your monitoring activity. Observation of established controls to monitor activity is not enough. They will always benefit from revision and improvement.

Why AML transparency is king on the international stage

Transparency is one of the pillars of good governance and it is transparency in the source of funds that deters criminals from trying to launder them through the world's financial systems, and encourages them to find more creative ways to launder their funds, for example in real estate or high-value goods, with the help of lawyers and accountants. This leads to regulatory scope-creep, as illustrated by the development of the European Union Money Laundering Directives in Chapter 1.

All AML activity, from the start of FATF to the most recent regulatory advances, is focused on establishing the source of funds that pass over national boundaries, onto the books or through the monetary system, as well as the end destination. Who is the ultimate owner of the value? Who will benefit from this transaction? Are they sanctioned by a relevant government authority, such as the US Office of Foreign Asset Control, the Trade and Industry Department of Hong Kong or the Australian Transaction Reports and Analysis Centre? Nations seeking to become more active on the international stage, such as China and Saudi Arabia, demonstrate their commitment to stamping out corruption within their countries by calling to account government officials and the very wealthy who consider themselves to be above the law.

Although giving little comfort when laws are used to further political objectives, taking action to reduce corruption gives an indication to the trading nations that it may be safe to allow transactions to pass into and through their jurisdictions without falling foul of AML regulations themselves. Essentially, by exposing corruption and money laundering by the elite of both governments and businesses, nations show themselves to be responsible actors on the international stage, as discussed in Chapter 5.

In AML terms, it is necessary to achieve transparency of the ownership of assets or value to be moved using the services of an obliged organization. Many resources are there to help AML professionals, giving a consistent message to nations as to how to minimize money laundering risk in their organizations. (See Chapter 1 for some useful website addresses for further research.)

> **Note**
>
> When implementing AML controls for cross-border activity, remember transparency is king on the international stage.

Client due diligence in risk assessment

In AML terms, client due diligence (CDD) is key in reducing risk. Your organizational risk assessment may already have several categories of CDD that give a clear indication of the levels of risk in different customer types as well as product, services and geography risks. Clear levels of CDD and enhanced due diligence (EDD) and measures to be taken with each control client risk, producing clear, auditable records of individual client activity, will provide you and your organization with proof of diligence in ensuring you know your clients. Aim to have enough evidence of AML compliance activity to show auditors and regulators your efforts in reducing organizational risk, then even if it is ultimately found to be lacking in some areas, sanctions are likely to be lighter. Where companies have found and remediated failures in their AML controls they are usually given credit by regulators.

Always ensure that the people carrying out the CDD know that they are responsible for providing clear, auditable records. Their training and support should keep them accountable for their activities, without allowing them to rely upon head office for day-to-day compliance. Oversight, yes; responsibility for knowing their clients, no.

Advantages and disadvantages of weak or strong regulators

Money launderers make good use of both weak and strong regulators, depending on their purpose. They may wish to create their wealth in jurisdictions where regulation is weak and where the focus on beneficial ownership is obfuscated, whether by a hierarchical, religious or autocratic regime. The cleaning of that wealth, always with the purpose of benefiting from it in safety, may well include moving it into a jurisdiction with a stronger regulatory culture, higher up the Transparency International Corruption Perceptions Index.

Weak regulators encourage organizations to push the boundaries of regulation in a downward spiral towards non-compliance, and where large sums of money are being moved there is the potential of high earnings for the organization handling it. Where the level of fines imposed for non-compliance are derisory, organizations may decide to run the risk of a case being brought against them and simply provisioning for the fine should it be imposed. Where fines dent profitability, there is a greater likelihood of future compliance, as in the case of Siemens in Case Study 3.1.

In other cases, fines imposed may not be sufficient to change behaviour, as with HSBC in Case Study 8.2. The same names do tend to recur and in 2017, following investigation of the 'Global laundromat', it was reported under the heading 'British banks handled vast sums of laundered Russian money' (*The Guardian*, 2017) that out of all the UK banks named, HSBC is said to have handled by far the most, at over US$545 million. A future study on how weak versus strong regulators impacted the activities of different players in the movement of this money is likely to make interesting reading!

Light-touch and potentially weaker regulatory environments tend also to encourage the use of offshore accounts to avoid paying taxes, such as those revealed in the Panama Papers of 2016 and the Paradise Papers of 2017. These exposed the placing of wealth in jurisdictions that require lower tax payments and where few questions are asked of its origin.

Navigating cultural change when implementing your AML strategy

Navigating cultural change when introducing AML requirements to an obliged entity calls for sufficient knowledge and skills, together with the self-assurance to enable the articulation of truth to power, as discussed in Chapter 8. Having the active support of the Chief Executive Officer and his or her team is essential in effecting cultural change. When complaints are made in high places because of the introduction of the AML risk management structure, you need to know that if you are acting within agreed parameters, and only putting in controls that are accepted and agreed by senior leadership, they will be steadfast in their support of your activity. Once middle management see that senior management are supportive, other managers will spare themselves the embarrassment of a failure to comply.

Hold the mind-set that challenge is really helpful when effecting cultural change, as the work to clarify and amend supporting policies and procedures will show your flexibility and commitment to the benefit of the organization, including the managers who the controls affect. If people are hostile but pay attention to the AML control environment, this shows their engagement. Your mission then is to turn them into allies.

Cultural change can be an extremely disruptive process but it does not have to be. If cultural change can be managed more slowly, the evolutionary effect is likely to be less dramatic. People will see why they must change the way they carry out their work in one area once they have seen improving changes in another, and the evolutionary approach tends to keep employees concentrating on their changed work rather than rebelling against it. Productivity is also part of risk management, so we need to keep AML professionals and the people they influence in the business focused on their work while the AML strategy embeds into working practices.

Closing comments

This book provides the basic tools to help you, an AML professional, reduce organizational risk in the area of money laundering.

Adopting a structured approach such as the one described in the AML strategy wheel will give your business leaders surety that the plan is well conceived, and if they have had the opportunity to influence its elements, they will be confident in its functionality. With your strategy including training and awareness, and the development of practical procedures, it is highly likely that business leaders will seek to draw on the skills of members of your AML team to help implement governance procedures of their own. That is success! Of course, regulations will change over time and new requirements will have to be implemented, so think to the future of your organization and your control environment when you make your AML plans a reality, as then you will come as close to future-proofing as possible within an articulate structure.

Even if you think that all of your efforts are no more than a drop in the ocean of the global AML compliance control environment, remember that it is a drop that would not be there without you, and drops gather together in streams on their way to the seas and oceans. The ocean may not be there without the effort you make. Take courage, and use your effective AML strategy to be the difference of sustainability in the world's economy and have an incremental cleaning effect in stamping out corruption and money laundering.

References

The Guardian (2017) British banks handled vast sums of laundered Russian money, available from: www.theguardian.com/world/2017/mar/20/british-banks-handled-vast-sums-of-laundered-russian-money (last accessed 24 January 2018)

https://www.fca.org.uk/firms/senior-managers-certification-regime (last accessed 18 January 2018)

INDEX

Note: key takeaways, references and further reading *and* 'stop and think' are indexed as such; page numbers in *italics* indicate figures or tables.